HAMLET:
WILLIAM SHAKESPEARE

HAMLET

By WILLIAM SHAKESPEARE

DESIGN BY DANIEL HABERMAN
ILLUSTRATIONS BY JACK WOLFGANG BECK

PUBLISHED BY
COMPOSING ROOM + GRAPHIC ARTS TYPOGRAPHERS, INC.
THOMPSON LITHOGRAPHIC ASSOCIATES INC.
FINCH, PRUYN & COMPANY, INC.
SENDOR BINDERY, INC.

INTRODUCTION—*A philosophical speculator*

Hamlet, by William Shakespeare, is the sixth in a
series of annual keepsakes for the friends of the publishers.

The tragedy of Hamlet, Prince of Denmark, is Shakespeare's best-
known play. Completed in 1601, the major tragedies of *Othello*,
Macbeth and *King Lear* were to follow. The plot of Hamlet is an ancient
one that tells of a relatively barbaric time; the narrative appearing as early as
the twelfth century in *Historica Danica*, by Saxo Grammaticus.

Our epilogue is by William Hazlitt, perhaps the best of Shakespearean
scholars, and is from Hazlitt's *The Characters of Shakespear's
Plays*, second edition, published in London in 1818. The Second
Quarto of 1604 and the First Folio of 1623 were used
as guides in the preparation of this book.

The publishers of this series are proud that *The Tempest* was
designated one of "the Fifty Best Books of the Year" for 1971 by the
American Institute of Graphic Arts. We are once again indebted to
Jack Wolfgang Beck, whose illustrations reflect sensitive
attention to the details of the play and whose
time was generously given.

Elsinore, Denmark. Circa 1300.

DRAMATIS PERSONAE

CLAUDIUS, *King of Denmark*

HAMLET, *Prince of Denmark*

POLONIUS, *Lord Chamberlain*

HORATIO, *friend to Hamlet*

LAERTES, *son to Polonius*

MARCELLUS, BARNARDO, *officers*

FRANCISCO, *a soldier*

REYNALDO, *servant to Polonius*

TWO CLOWNS, *gravediggers*

FORTINBRAS, *Prince of Norway*

GERTRUDE, *Queen of Denmark, mother to Hamlet*

OPHELIA, *daughter to Polonius*

GHOST *of Hamlet's father*

**VOLTEMAND, OSRIC, CORNELIUS,
ROSENKRANTZ, GUILDENSTERN,** *courtiers*

PLAYERS, PRIEST, NORWEGIAN CAPTAIN, OTHERS

ACT ONE

A GUARD PLATFORM OF THE CASTLE

[Enter Barnardo and Francisco]

Barnardo. Who's there?

Francisco. Nay, answer me. Stand and unfold yourself.

Barnardo. Long live the King!

Francisco. Barnardo?

Barnardo. He.

Francisco. You come most carefully upon your hour.

Barnardo. 'Tis now struck twelve. Get thee to bed, Francisco.

Francisco. For this relief much thanks. 'Tis bitter cold,
And I am sick at heart.

Barnardo. Have you had quiet guard?

Francisco.   Not a mouse stirring.

Barnardo. Well, good night.
If you do meet Horatio and Marcellus,
The rivals of my watch, bid them make haste.
[Enter Horatio and Marcellus]

Francisco. I think I hear them. Stand, ho! Who is there?

Horatio.	Friends to this ground.
Marcellus.	And liegemen to the Dane.
Francisco.	Give you good night.
Marcellus.	O, farewell, honest soldier.
	Who hath relieved you?
Francisco.	Barnardo hath my place.
	Give you good night.
	[*Exit*]
Marcellus.	Holla, Barnardo!
Barnardo.	Say—
	What, is Horatio there?
Horatio.	A piece of him.
Barnardo.	Welcome, Horatio. Welcome, good Marcellus.
Marcellus.	What, has this thing appeared again tonight?
Barnardo.	I have seen nothing.
Marcellus.	Horatio says 'tis but our fantasy,
	And will not let belief take hold of him
	Touching this dreaded sight twice seen of us;
	Therefore I have entreated him along
	With us to watch the minutes of this night,
	That, if again this apparition come,
	He may approve our eyes and speak to it.

Horatio.	Tush, tush, 'twill not appear.
Barnardo.	Sit down awhile,
	And let us once again assail your ears,
	That are so fortified against our story,
	What we have two nights seen.
Horatio.	Well, sit we down,
	And let us hear Barnardo speak of this.
Barnardo.	Last night of all,
	When yond same star that's westward from the pole
	Had made his course t' illume that part of heaven
	Where now it burns, Marcellus and myself,
	The bell then beating one—
	[*Enter Ghost*]
Marcellus.	Peace, break thee off. Look where it comes again.
Barnardo.	In the same figure like the king that's dead.
Marcellus.	Thou art a scholar; speak to it, Horatio.
Barnardo.	Looks 'a not like the king? Mark it, Horatio.
Horatio.	Most like: it harrows me with fear and wonder.

Barnardo.	It would be spoke to.
Marcellus.	Speak to it, Horatio.
Horatio.	What art thou that usurp'st this time of night,
	Together with that fair and warlike form
	In which the majesty of buried Denmark
	Did sometimes march? By heaven I charge thee, speak.
Marcellus.	It is offended.
Barnardo.	See, it stalks away.
Horatio.	Stay! Speak, speak. I charge thee, speak.
	{*Exit Ghost*}
Marcellus.	'Tis gone and will not answer.
Barnardo.	How now, Horatio? You tremble and look pale.
	Is not this something more than fantasy?
	What think you on't?
Horatio.	Before my God, I might not this believe
	Without the sensible and true avouch
	Of mine own eyes.
Marcellus.	Is it not like the King?

Horatio. As thou art to thyself.

Such was the very armor he had on

When he the ambitious Norway combated:

So frowned he once, when, in an angry parle,

He smote the sledded Polacks on the ice.

'Tis strange.

Marcellus. Thus twice before, and jump at this dead hour,

With martial stalk hath he gone by our watch.

Horatio. In what particular thought to work I know not;

But, in the gross and scope of my opinion,

This bodes some strange eruption to our state.

Marcellus. Good now, sit down, and tell me he that knows,

Why this same strict and most observant watch

So nightly toils the subject of the land,

And why such daily cast of brazen cannon

And foreign mart for implements of war,

Why such impress of shipwrights, whose sore task

Does not divide the Sunday from the week,

What might be toward that this sweaty haste

Doth make the night joint-laborer with the day?

Who is't that can inform me?

Horatio.   That can I.

At least the whisper goes so: our last king,
Whose image even but now appeared to us,
Was, as you know, by Fortinbras of Norway,
Thereto pricked on by a most emulate pride,
Dared to the combat; in which our valiant Hamlet
(For so this side of our known world esteemed him)
Did slay this Fortinbras, who, by a sealed compact
Well ratified by law and heraldry,
Did forfeit, with his life, all those his lands
Which he stood seized of, to the conqueror;
Against the which a moiety competent
Was gagèd by our King, which had returned
To the inheritance of Fortinbras,
Had he been vanquisher, as, by the same comart
And carriage of the article designed,
His fell to Hamlet. Now, sir, young Fortinbras,
Of unimprovèd mettle hot and full,

Hath in the skirts of Norway here and there
Sharked up a list of lawless resolutes,
For food and diet, to some enterprise
That hath a stomach in't; which is no other,
As it doth well appear unto our state,
But to recover of us by strong hand
And terms compulsatory, those foresaid lands
So by his father lost; and this, I take it,
Is the main motive of our preparations,
The source of this our watch, and the chief head
Of this posthaste and romage in the land.

Barnardo. I think it be no other but e'en so;
Well may it sort that this portentous figure
Comes armèd through our watch so like the King
That was and is the question of these wars.

Horatio.   A mote it is to trouble the mind's eye:
In the most high and palmy state of Rome,
A little ere the mightiest Julius fell,
The graves stood tenantless, and the sheeted dead
Did squeak and gibber in the Roman streets;
As stars with trains of fire and dews of blood,
Disasters in the sun; and the moist star,
Upon whose influence Neptune's empire stands,
Was sick almost to doomsday with eclipse.
And even the like precurse of feared events,
As harbingers preceding still the fates
And prologue to the omen coming on,
Have heaven and earth together demonstrated
Unto our climatures and countrymen.
        [Enter Ghost]
But soft, behold, lo where it comes again!
I'll cross it, though it blast me.—Stay, illusion.
If thou hast any sound or use of voice,
Speak to me.

If there be any good thing to be done
That may to thee do ease and grace to me,
Speak to me.
If thou art privy to thy country's fate,
Which happily foreknowing may avoid,
O, speak!
Or if thou hast uphoarded in thy life
Extorted treasure in the womb of earth,
For which, they say, you spirits oft walk in death,
     {The cock crows}
Speak of it. Stay and speak. Stop it, Marcellus.

Marcellus. Shall I strike at it with my partisan?

Horatio. Do, if it will not stand.

Barnardo.   'Tis here.

Horatio.   'Tis here.

     {Exit Ghost}

Marcellus. 'Tis gone.
We do it wrong, being so majestical,
To offer it the show of violence,
For it is as the air, invulnerable,
And our vain blows malicious mockery.

Barnardo. It was about to speak when the cock crew.

Horatio. And then it started, like a guilty thing
Upon a fearful summons. I have heard,
The cock, that is the trumpet to the morn,
Doth with his lofty and shrill-sounding throat
Awake the god of day, and at his warning,
Whether in sea or fire, in earth or air,
Th' extravagant and erring spirit hies
To his confine; and of the truth herein
This present object made probation.

Marcellus. It faded on the crowing of the cock.
Some say that ever 'gainst that season comes
Wherein our Savior's birth is celebrated,
This bird of dawning singeth all night long,
And then, they say, no spirit dare stir abroad,
The nights are wholesome, then no planets strike,
No fairy takes, nor witch hath power to charm:
So hallowed and so gracious is that time.

Horatio. So have I heard and do in part believe it.
But look, the morn in russet mantle clad
Walks o'er the dew of yon high eastward hill.
Break we our watch up, and by my advice
Let us impart what we have seen tonight
Unto young Hamlet, for upon my life
This spirit, dumb to us, will speak to him.
Do you consent we shall acquaint him with it,
As needful in our loves, fitting our duty?
Marcellus. Let's do't, I pray, and I this morning know
Where we shall find him most convenient.

{*Exeunt*}

SCENE II

WITHIN THE CASTLE

[Enter Claudius, King of Denmark, Gertrude
the Queen, Hamlet, old Polonius and his son
Laertes, Voltemand and Cornelius, cum aliis]

King.   Though yet of Hamlet our dear brother's death
The memory be green, and that it us befitted
To bear our hearts in grief, and our whole kingdom
To be contracted in one brow of woe,
Yet so far hath discretion fought with nature
That we with wisest sorrow think on him
Together with remembrance of ourselves.
Therefore our sometime sister, now our Queen,
Th' imperial jointress to this warlike state,
Have we, as 'twere, with a defeated joy,
With an auspicious and a dropping eye,
With mirth in funeral, and with dirge in marriage,
In equal scale weighing delight and dole,
Taken to wife. Nor have we herein barred

Your better wisdoms, which have freely gone
With this affair along. For all, our thanks.
Now follows that you know young Fortinbras,
Holding a weak supposal of our worth,
Or thinking by our late dear brother's death
Our state to be disjoint and out of frame,
Colleaguèd with this dream of his advantage,
He hath not failed to pester us with message,
Importing the surrender of those lands
Lost by his father, with all bands of law,
To our most valiant brother. So much for him.
Now for ourself and for this time of meeting.
Thus much the business is: we have here writ
To Norway, uncle of young Fortinbras—
Who, impotent and bedrid, scarcely hears
Of this his nephew's purpose—to suppress
His further gait herein, in that the levies,

The lists, and full proportions are all made
Out of his subject; and we here dispatch
You, good Cornelius, and you, Voltemand,
For bearers of this greeting to old Norway,
Giving to you no further personal power
To business with the King, more than the scope
Of these delated articles allow.
Farewell, and let your haste commend your duty.

Cornelius, Voltemand.   In that, and all things, will we show our duty.

King.   We doubt it nothing. Heartily farewell.

       [*Exit Voltemand and Cornelius*]

And now, Laertes, what's the news with you?
You told us of some suit. What is't, Laertes?
You cannot speak of reason to the Dane
And lose your voice. What wouldst thou beg, Laertes,
That shall not be my offer, not thy asking?
The head is not more native to the heart,
The hand more instrumental to the mouth,
Than is the throne of Denmark to thy father.
What wouldst thou have, Laertes?

Laertes.	My dread lord,
	Your leave and favor to return to France,
	From whence, though willingly I came to Denmark
	To show my duty in your coronation,
	Yet now I must confess, that duty done,
	My thoughts and wishes bend again toward France
	And bow them to your gracious leave and pardon.
King.	Have you your father's leave? What says Polonius?
Polonius.	He hath, my lord, wrung from me my slow leave
	By laborsome petition, and at last
	Upon his will I sealed my hard consent.
	I do beseech you give him leave to go.
King.	Take thy fair hour, Laertes. Time be thine,
	And thy best graces spend it at thy will.
	But now, my cousin Hamlet, and my son—
Hamlet.	[*Aside*] A little more than kin, and less than kind!
King.	How is it that the clouds still hang on you?
Hamlet.	Not so, my lord. I am too much in the sun.

Queen.	Good Hamlet, cast thy nighted color off,
	And let thine eye look like a friend on Denmark.
	Do not forever with thy vailèd lids
	Seek for thy noble father in the dust.
	Thou know'st 'tis common; all that lives must die,
	Passing through nature to eternity.
Hamlet.	Ay, madam, it is common.
Queen.	If it be,
	Why seems it so particular with thee?
Hamlet.	Seems, madam? Nay, it is. I know not "seems."
	'Tis not alone my inky cloak, good mother,
	Nor customary suits of solemn black,
	Nor windy suspiration of forced breath,
	No, nor the fruitful river in the eye,
	Nor the dejected havior of the visage,
	Together with all forms, moods, shapes of grief,
	That can denote me truly. These indeed seem,
	For they are actions that a man might play,
	But I have that within which passes show;
	These but the trappings and the suits of woe.

King. 'Tis sweet and commendable in your nature, Hamlet,
        To give these mourning duties to your father,
        But you must know your father lost a father,
        That father lost, lost his, and the survivor bound
        In filial obligation for some term
        To do obsequious sorrow. But to persevere
        In obstinate condolement is a course
        Of impious stubbornness. 'Tis unmanly grief.
        It shows a will most incorrect to heaven,
        A heart unfortified, a mind impatient,
        An understanding simple and unschooled.
        For what we know must be and is as common
        As any the most vulgar thing to sense,
        Why should we in our peevish opposition
        Take it to heart? Fie, 'tis a fault to heaven,
        A fault against the dead, a fault to nature,
        To reason most absurd, whose common theme
        Is death of fathers, and who still hath cried,
        From the first corse till he that died today,
    "This must be so." We pray you throw to earth
        This unprevailing woe, and think of us
        As of a father, for let the world take note

You are the most immediate to our throne,
And with no less nobility of love
Than that which dearest father bears his son
Do I impart toward you. For your intent
In going back to school in Wittenberg,
It is most retrograde to our desire,
And we beseech you, bend you to remain
Here in the cheer and comfort of our eye,
Our chiefest courtier, cousin, and our son.

Queen. Let not thy mother lose her prayers, Hamlet.
I pray thee stay with us, go not to Wittenberg.

Hamlet. I shall in all my best obey you, madam.

King. Why, 'tis a loving and a fair reply.
Be as ourself in Denmark. Madam, come.
This gentle and unforced accord of Hamlet
Sits smiling to my heart, in grace whereof
No jocund health that Denmark drinks today,
But the great cannon to the clouds shall tell,
And the King's rouse the heaven shall bruit again,
Respeaking earthly thunder. Come away.

[Flourish. Exeunt all but Hamlet]

Hamlet.　O that this too too solid flesh would melt,
　　　　　Thaw, and resolve itself into a dew,
　　　　　Or that the Everlasting had not fixed
　　　　　His canon 'gainst self-slaughter. O God, God,
　　　　　How weary, stale, flat, and unprofitable
　　　　　Seem to me all the uses of this world!
　　　　　Fie on't, ah, fie, 'tis an unweeded garden
　　　　　That grows to seed. Things rank and gross in nature
　　　　　Possess it merely. That it should come to this:
　　　　　But two months dead, nay, not so much, not two,
　　　　　So excellent a king, that was to this
　　　　　Hyperion to a satyr, so loving to my mother
　　　　　That he might not beteem the winds of heaven
　　　　　Visit her face too roughly. Heaven and earth,
　　　　　Must I remember? Why, she would hang on him
　　　　　As if increase of appetite had grown
　　　　　By what it fed on; and yet within a month—
　　　　　Let me not think on't; frailty, thy name is woman—
　　　　　A little month, or ere those shoes were old
　　　　　With which she followed my poor father's body
　　　　　Like Niobe, all tears, why she, even she—
　　　　　O God, a beast that wants discourse of reason

Would have mourned longer—married with my uncle,
My father's brother, but no more like my father
Than I to Hercules. Within a month,
Ere yet the salt of most unrighteous tears
Had left the flushing in her gallèd eyes,
She married. O, most wicked speed, to post
With such dexterity to incestuous sheets!
It is not, nor it cannot come to good.
But break my heart, for I must hold my tongue.
        [Enter Horatio, Marcellus, and Barnardo]

Horatio.   Hail to your lordship!

Hamlet.   I am glad to see you well.
        Horatio—or I do forget myself.

Horatio.   The same, my lord, and your poor servant ever.

Hamlet.   Sir, my good friend, I'll change that name with you.
        And what make you from Wittenberg, Horatio?
        Marcellus.

Marcellus.   My good lord!

Hamlet.   I am very glad to see you. *[To Barnardo]* Good even, sir.
        But what, in faith, make you from Wittenberg?

Horatio.   A truant disposition, good my lord.

Hamlet.	I would not hear your enemy say so,
	Nor shall you do my ear that violence
	To make it truster of your own report
	Against yourself. I know you are no truant.
	But what is your affair in Elsinore?
	We'll teach you to drink deep ere you depart.
Horatio.	My lord, I came to see your father's funeral.
Hamlet.	I prithee do not mock me, fellow student.
	I think it was to see my mother's wedding.
Horatio.	Indeed, my lord, it followed hard upon.
Hamlet.	Thrift, thrift, Horatio. The funeral baked meats
	Did coldly furnish forth the marriage tables.
	Would I had met my dearest foe in heaven
	Or ever I had seen that day, Horatio!
	My father, methinks I see my father.
Horatio.	Where, my lord?
Hamlet.	In my mind's eye, Horatio.
Horatio.	I saw him once. 'A was a goodly king.
Hamlet.	'A was a man, take him for all in all,
	I shall not look upon his like again.

Horatio.	My lord, I think I saw him yesternight.
Hamlet.	Saw? Who?
Horatio.	My lord, the King your father.
Hamlet.	The King my father?
Horatio.	Season your admiration for a while
	With an attent ear till I may deliver
	Upon the witness of these gentlemen
	This marvel to you.
Hamlet.	For God's love let me hear!
Horatio.	Two nights together had these gentlemen,
	Marcellus and Barnardo, on their watch
	In the dead waste and middle of the night
	Been thus encountered. A figure like your father,
	Armèd at point exactly, cap-a-pe,
	Appears before them, and with solemn march
	Goes slow and stately by them. Thrice he walked
	By their oppressed and fear-surprisèd eyes,
	Within his truncheon's length, whilst they, distilled
	Almost to jelly with the act of fear,
	Stand dumb and speak not to him. This to me
	In dreadful secrecy impart they did,

And I with them the third night kept the watch,
Where, as they had delivered, both in time,
Form of the thing, each word made true and good,
The apparition comes. I knew your father.
These hands are not more like.

Hamlet.   But where was this?

Marcellus. My lord, upon the platform where we watched.

Hamlet. Did you not speak to it?

Horatio.   My lord, I did;
But answer made it none. Yet once methought
It lifted up its head and did address
Itself to motion like as it would speak:
But even then the morning cock crew loud,
And at the sound it shrunk in haste away
And vanished from our sight.

Hamlet.   'Tis very strange.

Horatio. As I do live, my honored lord, 'tis true,
And we did think it writ down in our duty
To let you know of it.

Hamlet. Indeed, indeed, sirs, but this troubles me.
Hold you the watch tonight?

All.   We do, my lord.

Hamlet. Armed, say you?

All. Armed, my lord.

Hamlet. From top to toe?

All. My lord, from head to foot.

Hamlet. Then saw you not his face.

Horatio. O, yes, my lord. He wore his beaver up.

Hamlet. What, looked he frowningly?

Horatio. A countenance more in sorrow than in anger.

Hamlet. Pale or red?

Horatio. Nay, very pale.

Hamlet. And fixed his eyes upon you?

Horatio. Most constantly.

Hamlet. I would I had been there.

Horatio. It would have much amazed you.

Hamlet. Very like, very like. Stayed it long?

Horatio. While one with moderate haste might tell a hundred.

Both. Longer, longer.

Horatio. Not when I saw't.

Hamlet. His beard was grizzled, no?

Horatio.	It was as I have seen it in his life,
	A sable silvered.
Hamlet.	I will watch tonight.
	Perchance 'twill walk again.
Horatio.	I warr'nt it will.
Hamlet.	If it assume my noble father's person,
	I'll speak to it though hell itself should gape
	And bid me hold my peace. I pray you all,
	If you have hitherto concealed this sight,
	Let it be tenable in your silence still,
	And whatsomever else shall hap tonight,
	Give it an understanding but no tongue;
	I will requite your loves. So fare you well.
	Upon the platform 'twixt eleven and twelve
	I'll visit you.
All.	Our duty to your honor.
Hamlet.	Your loves, as mine to you. Farewell.

{*Exeunt all but Hamlet*}

My father's spirit—in arms? All is not well.

I doubt some foul play. Would the night were come!

Till then sit still, my soul. Foul deeds will rise,

Though all the earth o'erwhelm them, to men's eyes.

{*Exit*}

[Enter Laertes and Ophelia, his sister]

Laertes. My necessaries are embarked. Farewell.

And, sister, as the winds give benefit

And convoy is assistant, do not sleep,

But let me hear from you.

Ophelia.   Do you doubt that?

Laertes. For Hamlet, and the trifling of his favor,

Hold it a fashion and a toy in blood,

A violet in the youth of primy nature,

Forward, not permanent, sweet, not lasting,

The perfume and suppliance of a minute,

No more.

Ophelia.   No more but so?

Laertes.   Think it no more.

For nature crescent does not grow alone

In thews and bulk, but as this temple waxes,

The inward service of the mind and soul

Grows wide withal. Perhaps he loves you now,

And now no soil nor cautel doth besmirch
The virtue of his will; but you must fear,
His greatness weighed, his will is not his own.
For he himself is subject to his birth.
He may not, as unvalued persons do,
Carve for himself; for on his choice depends
The safety and health of this whole state;
And therefore must his choice be circumscribed
Unto the voice and yielding of that body
Whereof he is the head. Then if he says he loves you,
It fits your wisdom so far to believe it
As he in his particular act and place
May give his saying deed, which is no further
Than the main voice of Denmark goes withal.
Then weigh what loss your honor may sustain
If with too credent ear you list his songs,
Or lose your heart, or your chaste treasure open
To his unmastered importunity.
Fear it, Ophelia, fear it, my dear sister,
And keep you in the rear of your affection,

Out of the shot and danger of desire.

The chariest maid is prodigal enough

If she unmask her beauty to the moon.

Virtue itself scapes not calumnious strokes.

The canker galls the infants of the spring

Too oft before their buttons be disclosed,

And in the morn and liquid dew of youth

Contagious blastments are most imminent.

Be wary then; best safety lies in fear;

Youth to itself rebels, though none else near.

Ophelia. I shall the effect of this good lesson keep

As watchman to my heart, but, good my brother,

Do not, as some ungracious pastors do,

Show me the steep and thorny way to heaven,

Whiles, like a puffed and reckless libertine,

Himself the primrose path of dalliance treads

And recks not his own rede.

[*Enter Polonius*]

Laertes.   O, fear me not.
I stay too long. But here my father comes.
A double blessing is a double grace;
Occasion smiles upon a second leave.

Polonius.   Yet here, Laertes? Aboard, aboard, for shame!
The wind sits in the shoulder of your sail,
And you are stayed for. There—my blessing with thee,
And these few precepts in thy memory
Look thou character. Give thy thoughts no tongue,
Nor any unproportioned thought his act.
Be thou familiar, but by no means vulgar.
Those friends thou hast, and their adoption tried,
Grapple them unto thy soul with hoops of steel,
But do not dull thy palm with entertainment
Of each new-hatched, unfledged courage. Beware
Of entrance to a quarrel; but being in,
Bear't that th' opposèd may beware of thee.
Give every man thine ear, but few thy voice;

Take each man's censure, but reserve thy judgment.
Costly thy habit as thy purse can buy,
But not expressed in fancy; rich, not gaudy,
For the apparel oft proclaims the man,
And they in France of the best rank and station
Are of a most select and generous, chief in that.
Neither a borrower nor a lender be,
For loan oft loses both itself and friend,
And borrowing dulleth edge of husbandry.
This above all, to thine own self be true,
And it must follow, as the night the day,
Thou canst not then be false to any man.
Farewell. My blessing season this in thee!

Laertes. Most humbly do I take my leave, my lord.

Polonius. The time invites you. Go, your servants tend.

Laertes. Farewell, Ophelia, and remember well
What I have said to you.

Ophelia.   'Tis in my memory locked,
And you yourself shall keep the key of it.

Laertes.	Farewell.
	[Exit]
Polonius.	What is't, Ophelia, he hath said to you?
Ophelia.	So please you, something touching the Lord Hamlet.
Polonius.	Marry, well bethought.
	'Tis told me he hath very oft of late
	Given private time to you, and you yourself
	Have of your audience been most free and bounteous.
	If it be so—as so 'tis put on me,
	And that in way of caution—I must tell you
	You do not understand yourself so clearly
	As it behooves my daughter and your honor.
	What is between you? Give me up the truth.
Ophelia.	He hath, my lord, of late made many tenders
	Of his affection to me.
Polonius.	Affection pooh! You speak like a green girl,
	Unsifted in such perilous circumstance.
	Do you believe his tenders, as you call them?

Ophelia.	I do not know, my lord, what I should think.
Polonius.	Marry, I will teach you. Think yourself a baby
	That you have ta'en these tenders for true pay
	Which are not sterling. Tender yourself more dearly,
	Or (not to crack the wind of the poor phrase)
	Tend'ring it thus you'll tender me a fool.
Ophelia.	My lord, he hath importuned me with love
	In honorable fashion.
Polonius.	Ay, fashion you may call it. Go to, go to.
Ophelia.	And hath given countenance to his speech, my lord,
	With almost all the holy vows of heaven.
Polonius.	Ay, springes to catch woodcocks. I do know,
	When the blood burns, how prodigal the soul
	Lends the tongue vows. These blazes, daughter,
	Giving more light than heat, extinct in both,
	Even in their promise, as it is a-making,
	You must not take for fire. From this time
	Be something scanter of your maiden presence.
	Set your entreatments at a higher rate

Than a command to parley. For Lord Hamlet,
Believe so much in him that he is young,
And with a larger tether may he walk
Than may be given you. In few, Ophelia,
Do not believe his vows, for they are brokers,
Not of that dye which their investments show,
But mere implorators of unholy suits,
Breathing like sanctified and pious bonds,
The better to beguile. This is for all:
I would not, in plain terms, from this time forth
Have you so slander any moment leisure
As to give words or talk with the Lord Hamlet.
Look to't, I charge you. Come your ways.

Ophelia.   I shall obey, my lord.

    {Exeunt}

{*Enter Hamlet, Horatio, and Marcellus*}

Hamlet.   The air bites shrewdly; it is very cold.

Horatio.   It is a nipping and an eager air.

Hamlet.   What hour now?

Horatio.   I think it lacks of twelve.

Marcellus.   No, it is struck.

Horatio.   Indeed? I heard it not. It then draws near the season
Wherein the spirit held his wont to walk.

   {*A flourish of trumpets, and two pieces go off*}

What does this mean, my lord?

Hamlet.   The King doth wake tonight and takes his rouse,
Keeps wassail, and the swagg'ring upspring reels,
And as he drains his draughts of Rhenish down
The kettledrum and trumpet thus bray out
The triumph of his pledge.

Horatio.   Is it a custom?

Hamlet. Ay, marry, is't,
But to my mind, though I am native here
And to the manner born, it is a custom
More honored in the breach than the observance.
This heavy-headed revel east and west
Makes us traduced and taxed of other nations.
They clepe us drunkards and with swinish phrase
Soil our addition, and indeed it takes
From our achievements, though performed at height,
The pith and marrow of our attribute.
So oft it chances in particular men
That for some vicious mole of nature in them,
As in their birth, wherein they are not guilty,
(Since nature cannot choose his origin)
By the o'ergrowth of some complexion,
Oft breaking down the pales and forts of reason,
Or by some habit that too much o'erleavens
The form of plausive manners, that (these men,
Carrying, I say, the stamp of one defect,
Being nature's livery, or fortune's star)
Their virtues else, be they as pure as grace,

As infinite as man may undergo,
Shall in the general censure take corruption
From that particular fault. The dram of evil
Doth all the noble substance of a doubt,
To his own scandal.

     [*Enter Ghost*]

Horatio.   Look, my lord, it comes.
Hamlet. Angels and ministers of grace defend us!
Be thou a spirit of health or goblin damned,
Bring with thee airs from heaven or blasts from hell,
Be thy intents wicked or charitable,
Thou com'st in such a questionable shape
That I will speak to thee. I'll call thee Hamlet,
King, father, royal Dane. O, answer me!
Let me not burst in ignorance, but tell
Why thy canonized bones, hearsèd in death,
Have burst their cerements, why the sepulcher
Wherein we saw thee quietly interred
Hath oped his ponderous and marble jaws

To cast thee up again. What may this mean
That thou, dead corse, again in complete steel,
Revisits thus the glimpses of the moon,
Making night hideous, and we fools of nature
So horridly to shake our disposition
With thoughts beyond the reaches of our souls?
Say, why is this? Wherefore? What should we do?
　　　{Ghost beckons Hamlet}

Horatio.　It beckons you to go away with it,
As if it some impartment did desire
To you alone.

Marcellus.　　　　　　Look with what courteous action
It waves you to a more removèd ground.
But do not go with it.

Horatio.　　　　　　　　No, by no means.
Hamlet.　It will not speak. Then I will follow it.
Horatio.　Do not, my lord.

Hamlet.   Why, what should be the fear?
I do not set my life at a pin's fee,
And for my soul, what can it do to that,
Being a thing immortal as itself?
It waves me forth again. I'll follow it.

Horatio. What if it tempt you toward the flood, my lord.
Or to the dreadful summit of the cliff
That beetles o'er his base into the sea,
And there assume some other horrible form,
Which might deprive your sovereignty of reason
And draw you into madness? Think of it.
The very place puts toys of desperation,
Without more motive, into every brain
That looks so many fathoms to the sea
And hears it roar beneath.

Hamlet.   It waves me still.
Go on; I'll follow thee.

Marcellus. You shall not go, my lord.

Hamlet.   Hold off your hands.

Horatio.	Be ruled. You shall not go.
Hamlet.	My fate cries out
	And makes each petty artere in this body
	As hardy as the Nemean lion's nerve.
	Still am I called! Unhand me, gentlemen.
	By heaven, I'll make a ghost of him that lets me!
	I say, away! Go on. I'll follow thee.
	{Exit Ghost and Hamlet}
Horatio.	He waxes desperate with imagination.
Marcellus.	Let's follow. 'Tis not fit thus to obey him.
Horatio.	Have after! To what issue will this come?
Marcellus.	Something is rotten in the state of Denmark.
Horatio.	Heaven will direct it.
Marcellus.	Nay, let's follow him.
	{Exeunt}

SCENE V

THE BATTLEMENTS

[Enter Ghost and Hamlet]

Hamlet. Whither wilt thou lead me? Speak; I'll go no further.

Ghost. Mark me.

Hamlet.   I will.

Ghost.   My hour is almost come,
When I to sulf'rous and tormenting flames
Must render up myself.

Hamlet.   Alas, poor ghost.

Ghost. Pity me not, but lend thy serious hearing
To what I shall unfold.

Hamlet.   Speak. I am bound to hear.

Ghost. So art thou to revenge, when thou shalt hear.

Hamlet. What?

Ghost.	I am thy father's spirit,
	Doomed for a certain term to walk the night,
	And for the day confined to fast in fires,
	Till the foul crimes done in my days of nature
	Are burnt and purged away. But that I am forbid
	To tell the secrets of my prison house,
	I could a tale unfold whose lightest word
	Would harrow up thy soul, freeze thy young blood,
	Make thy two eyes like stars start from their spheres,
	Thy knotted and combinèd locks to part,
	And each particular hair to stand an end
	Like quills upon the fearful porpentine.
	But this eternal blazon must not be
	To ears of flesh and blood. List, list, O, list!
	If thou didst ever thy dear father love—
Hamlet.	O God!
Ghost.	Revenge his foul and most unnatural murder.

Hamlet.	Murder?
Ghost.	Murder most foul, as in the best it is,
	But this most foul, strange, and unnatural.
Hamlet.	Haste me to know't, that I, with wings as swift
	As meditation or the thoughts of love,
	May sweep to my revenge.
Ghost.	I find thee apt,
	And duller shouldst thou be than the fat weed
	That roots itself in ease on Lethe wharf,
	Wouldst thou not stir in this. Now, Hamlet, hear.
	'Tis given out that, sleeping in my orchard,
	A serpent stung me. So the whole ear of Denmark
	Is by a forgèd process of my death
	Rankly abused. But know, thou noble youth,
	The serpent that did sting thy father's life
	Now wears his crown.
Hamlet.	O my prophetic soul!
	My uncle?

Ghost.   Ay, that incestuous, that adulterate beast,
With witchcraft of his wits, with traitorous gifts—
O wicked wit and gifts, that have the power
So to seduce!—won to his shameful lust
The will of my most seeming-virtuous queen.
O Hamlet, what a falling-off was there,
From me, whose love was of that dignity
That it went hand in hand even with the vow
I made to her in marriage, and to decline
Upon a wretch whose natural gifts were poor
To those of mine.
But virtue, as it never will be moved,
Though lewdness court it in a shape of heaven,
So lust, though to a radiant angel linked,
Will sate itself in a celestial bed
And prey on garbage.
But soft, methinks I scent the morning air;

Brief let me be. Sleeping within my orchard,
My custom always of the afternoon,
Upon my secure hour thy uncle stole
With juice of cursed hebona in a vial,
And in the porches of my ears did pour
The leperous distillment, whose effect
Holds such an enmity with blood of man
That swift as quicksilver it courses through
The natural gates and alleys of the body,
And with a sudden vigor it doth posset
And curd, like eager droppings into milk,
The thin and wholesome blood. So did it mine,
And a most instant tetter barked about
Most lazarlike with vile and loathsome crust
All my smooth body.
Thus was I, sleeping, by a brother's hand
Of life, of crown, of queen at once dispatched,
Cut off even in the blossoms of my sin,

Unhouseled, disappointed, unaneled,
No reck'ning made, but sent to my account
With all my imperfections on my head.
O, horrible! O, horrible! Most horrible!
If thou hast nature in thee, bear it not.
Let not the royal bed of Denmark be
A couch for luxury and damnèd incest.
But howsomever thou pursues this act,
Taint not thy mind, nor let thy soul contrive
Against thy mother aught. Leave her to heaven
And to those thorns that in her bosom lodge
To prick and sting her. Fare thee well at once.
The glowworm shows the matin to be near
And 'gins to pale his uneffectual fire.
Adieu, adieu, adieu. Remember me.

{Exit}

Hamlet. O all you host of heaven! O earth! What else?
And shall I couple hell? O fie! Hold, hold, my heart,
And you, my sinews, grow not instant old,
But bear me stiffly up. Remember thee?
Ay, thou poor ghost, whiles memory holds a seat
In this distracted globe. Remember thee?
Yea, from the table of my memory
I'll wipe away all trivial fond records,
All saws of books, all forms, all pressures past
That youth and observation copied there,
And thy commandment all alone shall live
Within the book and volume of my brain,
Unmixed with baser matter. Yes, by heaven!
O most pernicious woman!
O villain, villain, smiling, damnèd villain!
My tables—meet it is I set it down
That one may smile, and smile, and be a villain.
At least I am sure it may be so in Denmark. {*Writes*}
So, uncle, there you are. Now to my word:
It is "Adieu, adieu, remember me."
I have sworn't.

Horatio, Marcellus.	{*Within*} My lord, my lord!
	{*Enter Horatio and Marcellus*}
Marcellus.	Lord Hamlet!
Horatio.	Heavens secure him!
Hamlet.	So be it!
Marcellus.	Illo, ho, ho, my lord!
Hamlet.	Hillo, ho, ho, boy! Come, bird, come.
Marcellus.	How is't, my noble lord?
Horatio.	What news, my lord?
Hamlet.	O, wonderful!
Horatio.	Good my lord, tell it.
Hamlet.	No, you will reveal it.
Horatio.	Not I, my lord, by heaven.
Marcellus.	Nor I, my lord.
Hamlet.	How say you then? Would heart of man once think it? But you'll be secret?
Both.	Ay, by heaven, my lord.
Hamlet.	There's never a villain dwelling in all Denmark But he's an arrant knave.

Horatio.   There needs no ghost, my lord, come from the grave
            To tell us this.

Hamlet.   Why, right, you are in the right;
            And so, without more circumstance at all,
            I hold it fit that we shake hands and part:
            You, as your business and desire shall point you,
            For every man hath business and desire
            Such as it is, and for my own poor part,
            Look you, I'll go pray.

Horatio.   These are but wild and whirling words, my lord.

Hamlet.   I am sorry they offend you, heartily;
            Yes, faith, heartily.

Horatio.   There's no offense, my lord.

Hamlet.   Yes, by Saint Patrick, but there is, Horatio,
            And much offense too. Touching this vision here,
            It is an honest ghost, that let me tell you.
            For your desire to know what is between us,
            O'ermaster't as you may. And now, good friends,
            As you are friends, scholars, and soldiers,
            Give me one poor request.

Horatio.	What is't, my lord? We will.
Hamlet.	Never make known what you have seen tonight.
Both.	My lord, we will not.
Hamlet.	Nay, but swear't.
Horatio.	In faith,

My lord, not I.

Marcellus.	Nor I, my lord—in faith.
Hamlet.	Upon my sword.
Marcellus.	We have sworn, my lord, already.
Hamlet.	Indeed, upon my sword, indeed.

        [Ghost cries under the stage]

Ghost.	Swear.
Hamlet.	Ha, ha, boy, say'st thou so? Art thou there, truepenny?

Come on. You hear this fellow in the cellarage.

Consent to swear.

Horatio.	Propose the oath, my lord.
Hamlet.	Never to speak of this that you have seen.

Swear by my sword.

Ghost.	*[Beneath]* Swear.

Hamlet.	*Hic et ubique?* Then we'll shift our ground;
	Come hither, gentlemen,
	And lay your hands again upon my sword.
	Swear by my sword
	Never to speak of this that you have heard.
Ghost.	{*Beneath*} Swear by his sword.
Hamlet.	Well said, old mole! Canst work i' th' earth so fast?
	A worthy pioner! Once more remove, good friends.
Horatio.	O day and night, but this is wondrous strange!
Hamlet.	And therefore as a stranger give it welcome.
	There are more things in heaven and earth, Horatio,
	Than are dreamt of in your philosophy.
	But come:
	Here as before, never, so help you mercy,
	How strange or odd some'er I bear myself
	(As I perchance hereafter shall think meet
	To put an antic disposition on),
	That you, at such times seeing me, never shall
	With arms encumb'red thus, or this headshake,

Or by pronouncing of some doubtful phrase,
As "Well, well, we know," or "We could, an if we would,"
Or "If we list to speak," or "There be, an if they might,"
Or such ambiguous giving out, to note
That you know aught of me—this do swear,
So grace and mercy at your most need help you.

Ghost. {*Beneath*} Swear.
        {*They swear*}
Hamlet. Rest, rest, perturbèd spirit. So, gentlemen,
With all my love I do commend me to you,
And what so poor a man as Hamlet is
May do t' express his love and friending to you,
God willing, shall not lack. Let us go in together,
And still your fingers on your lips, I pray.
The time is out of joint. O cursèd spite,
That ever I was born to set it right!
Nay, come, let's go together.
        {*Exeunt*}

ACT TWO

SCENE I

A ROOM AT ELSINORE

[Enter Polonius, with his man Reynaldo]

Polonius. Give him this money and these notes, Reynaldo.

Reynaldo. I will, my lord.

Polonius. You shall do marvell's wisely, good Reynaldo,
Before you visit him, to make inquire
Of his behavior.

Reynaldo. My lord, I did intend it.

Polonius. Marry, well said, very well said. Look you sir,
Inquire me first what Danskers are in Paris,
And how, and who, what means, and where they keep,
What company, at what expense; and finding
By this encompassment and drift of question
That they do know my son, come you more nearer
Than your particular demands will touch it.
Take you as 'twere some distant knowledge of him,
As thus, "I know his father and his friends,
And in part him." Do you mark this, Reynaldo?

Reynaldo.   Ay, very well, my lord.

Polonius.   "And in part him, but," you may say, "not well,
            But if't be he I mean, he's very wild,
            Addicted so and so." And there put on him
            What forgeries you please; marry, none so rank
            As may dishonor him—take heed of that—
            But, sir, such wanton, wild, and usual slips
            As are companions noted and most known
            To youth and liberty.

Reynaldo.   As gaming, my lord.

Polonius.   Ay, or drinking, fencing, swearing, quarreling,
            Drabbing. You may go so far.

Reynaldo.   My lord, that would dishonor him.

Polonius.   Faith, no, as you may season it in the charge.
            You must not put another scandal on him,
            That he is open to incontinency.
            That's not my meaning. But breathe his faults so quaintly
            That they may seem the taints of liberty,
            The flash and outbreak of a fiery mind,
            A savageness in unreclaimèd blood,
            Of general assault.

Reynaldo.	But, my good lord—
Polonius.	Wherefore should you do this?
Reynaldo.	Ay, my lord,

I would know that.

Polonius.	Marry, sir, here's my drift,

And I believe it is a fetch of warrant.
You laying these slight sullies on my son
As 'twere a thing a little soiled i' th' working,
Mark you,
Your party in converse, him you would sound,
Having ever seen in the prenominate crimes
The youth you breathe of guilty, be assured
He closes with you in this consequence:
"Good sir," or so, or "friend," or "gentleman"—
According to the phrase or the addition
Of man and country—

Reynaldo.	Very good, my lord.
Polonius.	And then, sir, does 'a this—'a does—

What was I about to say? By the mass, I was
about to say something! Where did I leave?

Reynaldo. At "closes in the consequence," at "friend or
so," and "gentleman."

Polonius. At "closes in the consequence"—Ay, marry!
He closes thus: "I know the gentleman;
I saw him yesterday, or t'other day,
Or then, or then, with such or such, and, as you say,
There was 'a gaming, there o'ertook in's rouse,
There falling out at tennis"; or perchance,
"I saw him enter such a house of sale,"
Videlicet, a brothel, or so forth.
See you now—
Your bait of falsehood take this carp of truth,
And thus do we of wisdom and of reach,
With windlasses and with assays of bias,
By indirections find directions out.
So, by my former lecture and advice,
Shall you my son. You have me, have you not?

Reynaldo. My lord, I have.

Polonius.   God bye ye, fare ye well.

Reynaldo. Good my lord.

Polonius.	Observe his inclination in yourself.
Reynaldo.	I shall, my lord.
Polonius.	And let him ply his music.
Reynaldo.	Well, my lord.
Polonius.	Farewell.

{*Exit Reynaldo. Enter Ophelia*}

How now, Ophelia, what's the matter?

Ophelia.	O my lord, my lord, I have been so affrighted!
Polonius.	With what, i' th' name of God?
Ophelia.	My lord, as I was sewing in my closet,
	Lord Hamlet, with his doublet all unbraced,
	No hat upon his head, his stockings fouled,
	Ungartered, and down-gyvèd to his ankle,
	Pale as his shirt, his knees knocking each other,
	And with a look so piteous in purport,
	As if he had been loosèd out of hell
	To speak of horrors—he comes before me.
Polonius.	Mad for thy love?
Ophelia.	My lord, I do not know,
	But truly I do fear it.
Polonius.	What said he?

Ophelia.	He took me by the wrist and held me hard;
	Then goes he to the length of all his arm,
	And with his other hand thus o'er his brow
	He falls to such perusal of my face
	As 'a would draw it. Long stayed he so.
	At last, a little shaking of mine arm,
	And thrice his head thus waving up and down,
	He raised a sigh so piteous and profound
	As it did seem to shatter all his bulk
	And end his being. That done, he lets me go,
	And, with his head over his shoulder turned,
	He seemed to find his way without his eyes,
	For out o' doors he went without their helps,
	And to the last bended their light on me.
Polonius.	Come, go with me. I will go seek the King.
	This is the very ecstasy of love,
	Whose violent property fordoes itself
	And leads the will to desperate undertakings
	As oft any passions under heaven
	That does afflict our natures. I am sorry.
	What, have you given him any hard words of late?

Ophelia. No, my good lord; but as you did command,
I did repel his letters and denied
His access to me.

Polonius.   That hath made him mad.
I am sorry that with better heed and judgment
I had not quoted him. I feared he did but trifle
And meant to wrack thee; but beshrew my jealousy.
By heaven, it is as proper to our age
To cast beyond ourselves in our opinions
As it is common for the younger sort
To lack discretion. Come, go we to the King.
This must be known, which, being kept close, might move
More grief to hide than hate to utter love.
Come.

    [Exeunt]

*[Enter King and Queen, Rosencrantz
and Guildenstern, and other courtiers]*

King.   Welcome, dear Rosencrantz and Guildenstern.

Moreover that we much did long to see you,

The need we have to use you did provoke

Our hasty sending. Something have you heard

Of Hamlet's transformation: so call it,

Sith nor th' exterior nor the inward man

Resembles that it was. What it should be,

More than his father's death, that thus hath put him

So much from th' understanding of himself,

I cannot dream of. I entreat you both

That, being of so young days brought up with him,

And sith so neighbored to his youth and havior,

That you vouchsafe your rest here in our court

Some little time, so by your companies

To draw him on to pleasures, and to gather

So much as from occasion you may glean,

Whether aught to us unknown afflicts him thus,

That opened lies within our remedy.

Queen. Good gentlemen, he hath much talked of you,
And sure I am, two men there is not living
To whom he more adheres. If it will please you
To show us so much gentry and good will
As to expend your time with us awhile
For the supply and profit of our hope,
Your visitation shall receive such thanks
As fits a king's remembrance.

Rosencrantz.   Both your Majesties
Might, by the sovereign power you have of us,
Put your dread pleasures more into command
Than to entreaty.

Guildenstern.   But we both obey,
And here give up ourselves in the full bent
To lay our service freely at your feet,
To be commanded.

King. Thanks, Rosencrantz and gentle Guildenstern.

Queen. Thanks, Guildenstern and gentle Rosencrantz.
And I beseech you instantly to visit
My too much changèd son. Go, some of you,
And bring these gentlemen where Hamlet is.

Guildenstern. Heavens make our presence and our practices
Pleasant and helpful to him!

Queen. Ay, amen!
*{Exeunt Rosencrantz and Guildenstern
with some Attendants. Enter Polonius]*

Polonius. Th' ambassadors from Norway, my good lord,
Are joyfully returned.

King. Thou still hast been the father of good news.

Polonius. Have I, my lord? Assure you, my good liege,
I hold my duty, as I hold my soul,
Both to my God and to my gracious king;
And I do think, or else this brain of mine
Hunts not the trail of policy so sure
As it hath used to do, that I have found
The very cause of Hamlet's lunacy.

King.	O, speak of that! That do I long to hear.
Polonius.	Give first admittance to th' ambassadors.
	My news shall be the fruit to that great feast.
King.	Thyself do grace to them and bring them in.
	{Exit Polonius}
	He tells me, my dear Gertrude, he hath found
	The head and source of all your son's distemper.
Queen.	I doubt it is no other but the main,
	His father's death and our o'erhasty marriage.
King.	Well, we shall sift him.
	{Enter Polonius, Voltemand, and Cornelius}
	Welcome, my good friends.
	Say, Voltemand, what from our brother Norway?
Voltemand.	Most fair return of greetings and desires.
	Upon our first, he sent out to suppress
	His nephew's levies, which to him appeared
	To be a preparation 'gainst the Polack;
	But better looked into, he truly found

It was against your Highness, whereat grieved,
That so his sickness, age, and impotence
Was falsely borne in hand, sends out arrests
On Fortinbras; which he, in brief, obeys,
Receives rebuke from Norway, and in fine,
Makes vow before his uncle never more
To give th' assay of arms against your Majesty.
Whereon old Norway, overcome with joy,
Gives him threescore thousand crowns in annual fee
And his commission to employ those soldiers,
So levied as before, against the Polack,
With an entreaty, herein further shown,
    [*Gives a paper*]
That it might please you to give quiet pass
Through your dominions for this enterprise,
On such regards of safety and allowance
As therein are set down.

King.   It likes us well;
And at our more considered time we'll read,
Answer, and think upon this business.
Meantime, we thank you for your well-took labor.
Go to your rest; at night we'll feast together.
Most welcome home!
                    [*Exeunt Ambassadors*]
Polonius.   This business is well ended.
My liege and madam, to expostulate
What majesty should be, what duty is,
Why day is day, night night, and time is time,
Were nothing but to waste night, day, and time.
Therefore, since brevity is the soul of wit,
And tediousness the limbs and outward flourishes,
I will be brief. Your noble son is mad.
Mad call I it, for, to define true madness,
What is't but to be nothing else but mad?
But let that go.
Queen.   More matter, with less art.

Polonius. Madam, I swear I use no art at all.
That he's mad, 'tis true: 'tis true 'tis pity,
And pity 'tis 'tis true—a foolish figure.
But farewell it, for I will use no art.
Mad let us grant him then; and now remains
That we find out the cause of this effect,
Or rather say, the cause of this defect,
For this effect defective comes by cause.
Thus it remains, and the remainder thus.
Perpend.
I have a daughter: have, while she is mine,
Who in her duty and obedience, mark,
Hath given me this. Now gather, and surmise.
     [*Reads the letter*]
          "To the celestial, and my soul's idol, the most
          beautified Ophelia"—
That's an ill phrase, a vile phrase; "beautified"
is a vile phrase. But you shall hear. Thus:
          "In her excellent white bosom, these, &c."
Queen. Came this from Hamlet to her?

Polonius. Good madam, stay awhile. I will be faithful.

    "Doubt thou the stars are fire,

    Doubt that the sun doth move;

    Doubt truth to be a liar,

    But never doubt I love.

    O dear Ophelia, I am ill at these numbers.

    I have not art to reckon my groans; but

    that I love thee best, O most best, believe

    it. Adieu. Thine evermore, most dear lady,

    whilst this machine is to him,

              HAMLET."

This in obedience hath my daughter shown me,

And more above hath his solicitings,

As they fell out by time, by means, and place,

All given to mine ear.

King.   But how hath she

Received his love?

Polonius.   What do you think of me?

King. As of a man faithful and honorable.

Polonius. I would fain prove so. But what might you think,
When I had seen this hot love on the wing
(As I perceived it, I must tell you that,
Before my daughter told me), what might you,
Or my dear Majesty your Queen here, think,
If I had played the desk or table book,
Or given my heart a winking, mute and dumb,
Or looked upon this love with idle sight?
What might you think? No, I went round to work
And my young mistress thus I did bespeak:
"Lord Hamlet is a prince, out of thy star.
This must not be." And then I prescripts gave her,
That she should lock herself from his resort,
Admit no messengers, receive no tokens.
Which done, she took the fruits of my advice,
And he, repellèd, a short tale to make,
Fell into a sadness, then into a fast,
Thence to a watch, thence into a weakness,
Thence to a lightness, and, by this declension,
Into the madness wherein now he raves,
And all we mourn for.

King.	Do you think 'tis this?
Queen.	It may be, very like.
Polonius.	Hath there been such a time, I would fain know that,
	That I have positively said " 'Tis so,"
	When it proved otherwise?
King.	Not that I know.
Polonius.	{*Pointing to his head and shoulder*}
	Take this from this, if this be otherwise.
	If circumstances lead me, I will find
	Where truth is hid, though it were hid indeed
	Within the center.
King.	How may we try it further?
Polonius.	You know sometimes he walks four hours together
	Here in the lobby.
Queen.	So he does indeed.
Polonius.	At such a time I'll loose my daughter to him.
	Be you and I behind an arras then.
	Mark the encounter. If he love her not,
	And be not from his reason fall'n thereon,
	Let me be no assistant for a state
	But keep a farm and carters.
King.	We will try it.

[*Enter Hamlet reading a book*]

Queen. But look where sadly the poor wretch comes reading.

Polonius. Away, I do beseech you both, away.

[*Exit King and Queen*]

I'll board him presently. O, give me leave.

How does my good Lord Hamlet?

Hamlet. Well, God-a-mercy.

Polonius. Do you know me, my lord?

Hamlet. Excellent well. You are a fishmonger.

Polonius. Not I, my lord.

Hamlet. Then I would you were so honest a man.

Polonius. Honest, my lord?

Hamlet. Ay, sir. To be honest, as this world goes, is to be one man picked out of ten thousand.

Polonius. That's very true, my lord.

Hamlet. For if the sun breed maggots in a dead dog, being a good kissing carrion — Have you a daughter?

Polonius. I have, my lord.

Hamlet. Let her not walk i' th' sun. Conception is a blessing, but as your daughter may conceive, friend, look to't.

Polonius. [*Aside*] How say you by that? Still harping on my daughter. Yet he knew me not at first. 'A said I was a fishmonger. 'A is far gone, far gone. And truly in my youth I suffered much extremity for love, very near this. I'll speak to him again.—What do you read, my lord?

Hamlet. Words, words, words.

Polonius. What is the matter, my lord?

Hamlet. Between who?

Polonius. I mean the matter that you read, my lord.

Hamlet. Slanders, sir; for the satirical rogue says here that old men have gray beards, that their faces are wrinkled, their eyes purging thick amber and plum-tree gum, and that they have a plentiful lack of wit, together with most weak hams. All which, sir, though I most powerfully and potently believe, yet I hold it not honesty to have it thus set down; for you yourself, sir, should be old as I am if, like a crab, you could go backward.

Polonius. [*Aside*] Though this be madness, yet there is method in't. Will you walk out of the air, my lord?

Hamlet. Into my grave.

Polonius. Indeed, that's out of the air. [*Aside*] How pregnant sometimes his replies are! A happiness that often madness hits on, which reason and sanity could not so prosperously be delivered of. I will leave him and suddenly contrive the means of meeting between him and my daughter.—My lord, I will take my leave of you.

Hamlet. You cannot take from me anything that I will more willingly part withal—except my life, except my life, except my life.

[*Enter Guildenstern and Rosencrantz*]

Polonius. Fare you well, my lord.

Hamlet. These tedious old fools!

Polonius. You go to seek the Lord Hamlet? There he is.

Rosencrantz. [*To Polonius*] God save you, sir!

[*Exit Polonius*]

Guildenstern.	My honored lord!
Rosencrantz.	My most dear lord!
Hamlet.	My excellent good friends! How dost thou, Guildenstern? Ah, Rosencrantz! Good lads, how do you both?
Rosencrantz.	As the indifferent children of the earth.
Guildenstern.	Happy in that we are not overhappy. On Fortune's cap we are not the very button.
Hamlet.	Nor the soles of her shoe?
Rosencrantz.	Neither, my lord.
Hamlet.	Then you live about her waist, or in the middle of her favors?
Guildenstern.	Faith, her privates we.
Hamlet.	In the secret parts of Fortune? O, most true! She is a strumpet. What news?
Rosencrantz.	None, my lord, but that the world's grown honest.
Hamlet.	Then is doomsday near. But your news is not true. Let me question more in particular. What have you, my good friends, deserved at the hands of Fortune that she sends you to prison hither?

Guildenstern.	Prison, my lord?
Hamlet.	Denmark's a prison.
Rosencrantz.	Then is the world one.
Hamlet.	A goodly one, in which there are many confines, wards, and dungeons, Denmark being one o' th' worst.
Rosencrantz.	We think not so, my lord.
Hamlet.	Why, then 'tis none to you, for there is nothing either good or bad but thinking makes it so. To me it is a prison.
Rosencrantz.	Why then your ambition makes it one. 'Tis too narrow for your mind.
Hamlet.	O God, I could be bounded in a nutshell and count myself a king of infinite space, were it not that I have bad dreams.
Guildenstern.	Which dreams indeed are ambition, for the very substance of the ambitious is merely the shadow of a dream.
Hamlet.	A dream itself is but a shadow.

Rosencrantz.	Truly, and I hold ambition of so airy and light a quality that it is but a shadow's shadow.
Hamlet.	Then are our beggars bodies, and our monarchs and outstretched heroes the beggars' shadows. Shall we to th' court? For, by my fay, I cannot reason.
Both.	We'll wait upon you.
Hamlet.	No such matter. I will not sort you with the rest of my servants, for, to speak to you like an honest man, I am most dreadfully attended. But in the beaten way of friendship, what make you at Elsinore?
Rosencrantz.	To visit you, my lord; no other occasion.
Hamlet.	Beggar that I am, I am even poor in thanks, but I thank you; and sure, dear friends, my thanks are too dear a halfpenny. Were you not sent for? Is it your own inclining? Is it a free visitation? Come, come, deal justly with me. Come, come; nay, speak.
Guildenstern.	What should we say, my lord?

Hamlet.	Why anything—but to th' purpose. You were sent for, and there is a kind of confession in your looks, which your modesties have not craft enough to color. I know the good King and Queen have sent for you.
Rosencrantz.	To what end, my lord?
Hamlet.	That you must teach me. But let me conjure you by the rights of our fellowship, by the consonancy of our youth, by the obligation of our ever preserved love, and by what more dear a better proposer can charge you withal, be even and direct with me, whether you were sent for or no.
Rosencrantz.	[*Aside to Guildenstern*] What say you?
Hamlet.	[*Aside*] Nay then, I have an eye of you.—If you love me, hold not off.
Guildenstern.	My lord, we were sent for.

Hamlet. I will tell you why; so shall my anticipation prevent your discovery, and your secrecy to the King and Queen molt no feather. I have of late, but wherefore I know not, lost all my mirth, forgone all custom of exercises; and indeed, it goes so heavily with my disposition that this goodly frame, the earth, seems to me a sterile promontory; this most excellent canopy, the air, look you, this brave o'erhanging firmament, this majestical roof fretted with golden fire: why, it appeareth nothing to me but a foul and pestilent congregation of vapors. What a piece of work is a man, how noble in reason, how infinite in faculties, in form and moving how express and admirable, in action how like an angel, in apprehension how like a god: the beauty of the world, the paragon of animals; and yet to me, what is this quintessence of dust? Man delights not me; nor woman neither, though by your smiling you seem to say so.

Rosencrantz.	My lord, there was no such stuff in my thoughts.
Hamlet.	Why did ye laugh then, when I said "Man delights not me"?
Rosencrantz.	To think, my lord, if you delight not in man, what lenten entertainment the players shall receive from you. We coted them on the way, and hither are they coming to offer you service.
Hamlet.	He that plays the king shall be welcome; his Majesty shall have tribute of me; the adventurous knight shall use his foil and target; the lover shall not sigh gratis; the humorous man shall end his part in peace; the clown shall make those laugh whose lungs are tickle o' th' sere; and the lady shall say her mind freely, or the blank verse shall halt for't. What players are they?
Rosencrantz.	Even those you were wont to take such delight in, the tragedians of the city.
Hamlet.	How chances it they travel? Their residence, both in reputation and profit, was better both ways.

Rosencrantz.	I think their inhibition comes by the means of the late innovation.
Hamlet.	Do they hold the same estimation they did when I was in the city? Are they so followed?
Rosencrantz.	No indeed, are they not.
Hamlet.	How comes it? Do they grow rusty?
Rosencrantz.	Nay, their endeavor keeps in the wonted pace, but there is, sir, an eyrie of children, little eyases, that cry out on the top of question and are most tyrannically clapped for't. These are now the fashion, and so berattle the common stages (so they call them) that many wearing rapiers are afraid of goosequills and dare scarce come thither.
Hamlet.	What, are they children? Who maintains 'em? How are they escoted? Will they pursue the quality no longer than they can sing? Will they not say afterwards, if they should grow themselves to common players (as it is most like, if their means are no better), their writers do them wrong to make them exclaim against their own succession?

Rosencrantz. Faith, there has been much to-do on both sides, and the nation holds it no sin to tarre them to controversy. There was, for a while, no money bid for argument unless the poet and the player went to cuffs in the question.

Hamlet. Is't possible?

Guildenstern. O, there has been much throwing about of brains.

Hamlet. Do the boys carry it away?

Rosencrantz. Ay, that they do, my lord—Hercules and his load too.

Hamlet. It is not very strange, for my uncle is King of Denmark, and those that would make mouths at him while my father lived give twenty, forty, fifty, a hundred ducats apiece for his picture in little. 'Sblood, there is something in this more than natural, if philosophy could find it out.

[*A flourish*]

Guildenstern. There are the players.

Hamlet. Gentlemen, you are welcome to Elsinore. Your hands, come then. Th' appurtenance of welcome is fashion and ceremony. Let me comply with you in this garb, lest my extent to the players (which I tell you must show fairly outwards) should more appear like entertainment than yours. You are welcome. But my uncle-father and aunt-mother are deceived.

Guildenstern. In what, my dear lord?

Hamlet. I am but mad north-northwest: when the wind is southerly I know a hawk from a handsaw.

{Enter Polonius}

Polonius. Well be with you, gentlemen.

Hamlet. Hark you, Guildenstern, and you too; at each ear a hearer. That great baby you see there is not yet out of his swaddling clouts.

Rosencrantz. Happily he is the second time come to them, for they say an old man is twice a child.

Hamlet. I will prophesy he comes to tell me of the players. Mark it.—You say right, sir; a Monday morning, 'twas then indeed.

Polonius. My lord, I have news to tell you.

Hamlet.	My lord, I have news to tell you. When Roscius was an actor in Rome—
Polonius.	The actors are come hither, my lord.
Hamlet.	Buzz, buzz.
Polonius.	Upon my honor—
Hamlet.	Then came each actor on his ass—
Polonius.	The best actors in the world, either for tragedy, comedy, history, pastoral, pastoral-comical, historical-pastoral, tragical-historical, tragical-comical-historical-pastoral; scene individable, or poem unlimited. Seneca cannot be too heavy, nor Plautus too light. For the law of writ and the liberty, these are the only men.
Hamlet.	O Jeptha, judge of Israel, what a treasure hadst thou!
Polonius.	What a treasure had he, my lord?
Hamlet.	Why,

> "One fair daughter, and no more,
>   The which he lovèd passing well."

Polonius.	[*Aside*] Still on my daughter.
Hamlet.	Am I not i' th' right, old Jeptha?
Polonius.	If you call me Jeptha, my lord, I have a daughter that I love passing well.

Hamlet.	Nay, that follows not.
Polonius.	What follows then, my lord?
Hamlet.	Why, "As by lot, God wot," and then, you know, "It came to pass, as most like it was." The first row of the pious chanson will show you more, for look where my abridgment comes.

{*Enter the Players*}

You are welcome, masters, welcome, all. I am glad to see thee well. Welcome, good friends. O, old friend, why, thy face is valanced since I saw thee last. Com'st thou to beard me in Denmark? What, my young lady and mistress? By'r Lady, your ladyship is nearer to heaven than when I saw you last by the altitude of a chopine. Pray God your voice, like a piece of uncurrent gold, be not cracked within the ring.—Masters, you are all welcome. We'll e'en to't like French falconers, fly at anything we see. We'll have a speech straight. Come, give us a taste of your quality. Come, a passionate speech.

Player. What speech, my good lord?

Hamlet. I heard thee speak me a speech once, but it was never acted, or if it was, not above once, for the play, I remember, pleased not the million; 'twas caviary to the general, but it was (as I received it, and others, whose judgments in such matters cried in the top of mine) an excellent play, well digested in the scenes, set down with as much modesty as cunning. I remember one said there were no sallets in the lines to make the matter savory; nor no matter in the phrase that might indict the author of affectation, but called it an honest method, as wholesome as sweet, and by very much more handsome than fine. One speech in't I chiefly loved. 'Twas Aeneas' tale to Dido, and thereabout of it especially when he speaks of Priam's slaughter. If it live in your memory, begin at this line—let me see, let me see:

"The rugged Pyrrhus, like th' Hyrcanian beast—"
'Tis not so; it begins with Pyrrhus:

"The rugged Pyrrhus, he whose sable arms,
Black as his purpose, did the night resemble
When he lay couchèd in th' ominous horse,
Hath now this dread and black complexion smeared
With heraldry more dismal. Head to foot
Now is he total gules, horridly tricked
With blood of fathers, mothers, daughters, sons,
Baked and impasted with the parching streets,
That lend a tyrannous and a damnèd light
To their lord's murder. Roasted in wrath and fire,
And thus o'ersizèd with coagulate gore,
With eyes like carbuncles, the hellish Pyrrhus
Old grandsire Priam seeks."

So proceed you.

Polonius. Fore God, my lord, well spoken, with good accent and good discretion.

Player.   "Anon he finds him,
Striking too short at Greeks. His antique sword,
Rebellious to his arm, lies where it falls,
Repugnant to command. Unequal matched,
Pyrrhus at Priam drives, in rage strikes wide,
But with the whiff and wind of his fell sword
Th' unnervèd father falls. Then senseless Ilium,
Seeming to feel this blow, with flaming top
Stoops to his base, and with a hideous crash
Takes prisoner Pyrrhus' ear. For lo, his sword,
Which was declining on the milky head
Of reverend Priam, seemed i' th' air to stick.
So as a painted tyrant Pyrrhus stood,
And like a neutral to his will and matter
Did nothing.
But as we often see, against some storm,
A silence in the heavens, the rack stand still,
The bold winds speechless, and the orb below
As hush as death, anon the dreadful thunder
Doth rend the region, so after Pyrrhus' pause,

A rousèd vengeance sets him new awork,
And never did the Cyclops' hammers fall
On Mars's armor, forged for proof eterne,
With less remorse than Pyrrhus' bleeding sword
Now falls on Priam.
Out, out, thou strumpet Fortune! All you gods,
In general synod take away her power,
Break all the spokes and fellies from her wheel,
And bowl the round nave down the hill of heaven,
As low as to the fiends."

Polonius. This is too long.

Hamlet. It shall to the barber's, with your beard.—
Prithee say on. He's for a jig or a tale of bawdry,
or he sleeps. Say on; come to Hecuba.

Player. "But who (ah woe!) had seen the mobled queen—"

Hamlet. "The mobled queen"?

Polonius. That's good. "Mobled queen" is good.

Player. "Run barefoot up and down, threat'ning the flames

With bisson rheum; a clout upon that head

Where late the diadem stood, and for a robe,

About her lank and all o'erteemèd loins,

A blanket in the alarm of fear caught up—

Who this had seen, with tongue in venom steeped

'Gainst Fortune's state would treason have pronounced.

But if the gods themselves did see her then,

When she saw Pyrrhus make malicious sport

In mincing with his sword her husband's limbs,

The instant burst of clamor that she made

(Unless things mortal move them not at all)

Would have made milch the burning eyes of heaven

And passion in the gods."

Polonius. Look, whe'r he has not turned his color, and

has tears in's eyes. Prithee no more.

Hamlet. 'Tis well, I'll have thee speak out the rest of this

soon. Good my lord, will you see the players

well bestowed? Do you hear? Let them be well used, for they are the abstract and brief chronicles of the time. After your death you were better have a bad epitaph than their ill report while you live.

Polonius. My lord, I will use them according to their desert.

Hamlet. God's bodkin, man, much better! Use every man after his desert, and who shall scape whipping? Use them after your own honor and dignity. The less they deserve, the more merit is in your bounty. Take them in.

Polonius. Come, sirs.

Hamlet. Follow him, friends. We'll hear a play tomorrow. [Aside to Player] Dost thou hear me, old friend? Can you play The Murder of Gonzago?

Player. Ay, my lord.

Hamlet. We'll ha't tomorrow night. You could for a need study a speech of some dozen or sixteen lines which I would set down and insert in't, could you not?

Player.	Ay, my lord.
Hamlet.	Very well. Follow that lord, and look you mock him not. My good friends, I'll leave you till night. You are welcome to Elsinore.

{Exeunt Polonius and Players}

Rosencrantz.	Good my lord.

{Exeunt Rosencrantz and Guildenstern}

Hamlet.	Ay, so, God bye to you.—Now I am alone.
	O, what a rogue and peasant slave am I!
	Is it not monstrous that this player here,
	But in a fiction, in a dream of passion,
	Could force his soul so to his own conceit
	That from her working all his visage wanned,
	Tears in his eyes, distraction in his aspect,
	A broken voice, and his whole function suiting
	With forms to his conceit? And all for nothing!
	For Hecuba!
	What's Hecuba to him, or he to Hecuba,

That he should weep for her? What would he do
Had he the motive and the cue for passion
That I have? He would drown the stage with tears
And cleave the general ear with horrid speech,
Make mad the guilty and appall the free,
Confound the ignorant, and amaze indeed
The very faculties of eyes and ears. Yet I,
A dull and muddy-mettled rascal, peak
Like John-a-dreams, unpregnant of my cause,
And can say nothing. No, not for a king,
Upon whose property and most dear life
A damned defeat was made. Am I a coward?
Who calls me villain? Breaks my pate across?
Plucks off my beard and blows it in my face?
Tweaks me by the nose? Gives me the lie i' th' throat
As deep as to the lungs? Who does me this?
Ha, 'swounds, I should take it, for it cannot be
But I am pigeon-livered and lack gall
To make oppression bitter, or ere this

I should ha' fatted all the region kites
With this slave's offal. Bloody, bawdy villain!
Remorseless, treacherous, lecherous, kindless villain!
O, vengeance!
Why, what an ass am I! This is most brave,
That I, the son of a dear father murdered,
Prompted to my revenge by heaven and hell,
Must, like a whore, unpack my heart with words
And fall a-cursing like a very drab,
A stallion! Fie upon't, foh! About, my brains.
I have heard that guilty creatures sitting at a play
Have by the very cunning of the scene
Been struck so to the soul that presently
They have proclaimed their malefactions.
For murder, though it have no tongue, will speak
With most miraculous organ. I'll have these players
Play something like the murder of my father
Before mine uncle. I'll observe his looks,

I'll tent him to the quick. If 'a do blench,
I know my course. The spirit that I have seen
May be a devil, and the devil hath power
T' assume a pleasing shape, yea, and perhaps
Out of my weakness and my melancholy,
As he is very potent with such spirits,
Abuses me to damn me. I'll have grounds
More relative than this. The play's the thing
Wherein I'll catch the conscience of the King.

    {Exit}

ACT THREE

[*Enter King, Queen, Polonius, Ophelia,*
Rosencrantz, Guildenstern, and Lords]

King. And can you by no drift of conference
Get from him why he puts on this confusion,
Grating so harshly all his days of quiet
With turbulent and dangerous lunacy?

Rosencrantz. He does confess he feels himself distracted,
But from what cause 'a will by no means speak.

Guildenstern. Nor do we find him forward to be sounded,
But with a crafty madness keeps aloof
When we would bring him on to some confession
Of his true state.

Queen.   Did he receive you well?

Rosencrantz. Most like a gentleman.

Guildenstern. But with much forcing of his disposition.

Rosencrantz. Niggard of question, but of our demands
Most free in his reply.

Queen.   Did you assay him

To any pastime?

Rosencrantz.   Madam, it so fell out that certain players

We o'erraught on the way; of these we told him,

And there did seem in him a kind of joy

To hear of it. They are here about the court,

And, as I think, they have already order

This night to play before him.

Polonius.   'Tis most true,

And he beseeched me to entreat your Majesties

To hear and see the matter.

King.   With all my heart, and it doth much content me

To hear him so inclined.

Good gentlemen, give him a further edge

And drive his purpose into these delights.

Rosencrantz.   We shall, my lord.

{Exeunt Rosencrantz and Guildenstern}

King.   Sweet Gertrude, leave us too,
For we have closely sent for Hamlet hither,
That he, as 'twere by accident, may here
Affront Ophelia.
Her father and myself (lawful espials)
Will so bestow ourselves that, seeing unseen,
We may of their encounter frankly judge
And gather by him, as he is behaved,
If't be th' affliction of his love or no
That thus he suffers for.

Queen.   I shall obey you.
And for your part, Ophelia, I do wish
That your good beauties be the happy cause
Of Hamlet's wildness. So shall I hope your virtues
Will bring him to his wonted way again,
To both your honors.

Ophelia.   Madam, I wish it may.

        [Exit Queen]

Polonius.	Ophelia, walk you here.—Gracious, so please you,
	We will bestow ourselves. [*To Ophelia*] Read on this book,
	That show of such an exercise may color
	Your loneliness. We are oft to blame in this,
	'Tis too much proved, that with devotion's visage
	And pious action we do sugar o'er
	The devil himself.
King.	[*Aside*] O, 'tis too true.
	How smart a lash that speech doth give my conscience!
	The harlot's cheek, beautied with plast'ring art,
	Is not more ugly to the thing that helps it
	Than is my deed to my most painted word.
	O heavy burden!
Polonius.	I hear him coming. Let's withdraw, my lord.
	[*Exeunt King and Polonius, enter Hamlet*]
Hamlet.	To be, or not to be: that is the question:
	Whether 'tis nobler in the mind to suffer
	The slings and arrows of outrageous fortune,
	Or to take arms against a sea of troubles,
	And by opposing end them. To die, to sleep—
	No more—and by a sleep to say we end
	The heartache, and the thousand natural shocks
	That flesh is heir to! 'Tis a consummation

Devoutly to be wished. To die, to sleep—
To sleep—perchance to dream: ay, there's the rub,
For in that sleep of death what dreams may come
When we have shuffled off this mortal coil,
Must give us pause. There's the respect
That makes calamity of so long life:
For who would bear the whips and scorns of time,
Th' oppressor's wrong, the proud man's contumely,
The pangs of despised love, the law's delay,
The insolence of office, and the spurns
That patient merit of th' unworthy takes,
When he himself might his quietus make
With a bare bodkin? Who would fardels bear,
To grunt and sweat under a weary life,
But that the dread of something after death,
The undiscovered country, from whose bourn
No traveler returns, puzzles the will,
And makes us rather bear those ills we have,
Than fly to others that we know not of?
Thus conscience does make cowards of us all,
And thus the native hue of resolution

Is sicklied o'er with the pale cast of thought,
And enterprises of great pitch and moment,
With this regard their currents turn awry,
And lose the name of action.—Soft you now,
The fair Ophelia!—Nymph, in thy orisons
Be all my sins remembered.

Ophelia.   Good my lord,
How does your honor for this many a day?

Hamlet. I humbly thank you; well, well, well.

Ophelia. My lord, I have remembrances of yours
That I have longèd long to redeliver.
I pray you now, receive them.

Hamlet.   No, not I,
I never gave you aught.

Ophelia. My honored lord, you know right well you did,
And with them words of so sweet breath composed
As made these things more rich. Their perfume lost,
Take these again, for to the noble mind
Rich gifts wax poor when givers prove unkind.
There, my lord.

Hamlet. Ha, ha! Are you honest?

Ophelia. My lord?

Hamlet. Are you fair?

Ophelia. What means your lordship?

Hamlet. That if you be honest and fair, your honesty should admit no discourse to your beauty.

Ophelia. Could beauty, my lord, have better commerce than with honesty?

Hamlet. Ay, truly; for the power of beauty will sooner transform honesty from what it is to a bawd than the force of honesty can translate beauty into his likeness. This was sometime a paradox, but now the time gives it proof. I did love you once.

Ophelia. Indeed, my lord, you made me believe so.

Hamlet. You should not have believed me, for virtue cannot so inoculate our old stock but we shall relish of it. I loved you not.

Ophelia. I was the more deceived.

Hamlet. Get thee to a nunnery. Why wouldst thou be a breeder of sinners? I am myself indifferent honest, but yet I could accuse me of such things that it were better my mother had not borne me: I am very proud, revengeful, ambitious, with more offenses at my beck than I have thoughts to put them in, imagination to give them shape, or time to act them in. What should such fellows as I do crawling between earth and heaven? We are arrant knaves all; believe none of us. Go thy ways to a nunnery. Where's your father?

Ophelia. At home, my lord.

Hamlet. Let the doors be shut upon him, that he may play the fool nowhere but in's own house. Farewell.

Ophelia. O help him, you sweet heavens!

Hamlet. If thou dost marry, I'll give thee this plague for thy dowry: be thou as chaste as ice, as pure as snow, thou shalt not escape calumny. Get thee to a nunnery. Go, farewell. Or if thou wilt needs marry, marry a fool, for wise men know well enough what monsters you make of them. To a nunnery, go, and quickly too. Farewell.

Ophelia. Heavenly powers, restore him!

Hamlet. I have heard of your paintings, well enough. God hath given you one face, and you make yourselves another. You jig and amble, and you lisp; you nickname God's creatures and make your wantonness your ignorance. Go to, I'll no more on't; it hath made me mad. I say we will have no moe marriage. Those that are married already—all but one—shall live. The rest shall keep as they are. To a nunnery, go.

    [Exit]

Ophelia. O what a noble mind is here o'erthrown!

The courtier's, soldier's, scholar's, eye, tongue, sword,

Th' expectancy and rose of the fair state,

The glass of fashion, and the mold of form,

Th' observed of all observers, quite, quite down!

And I, of ladies most deject and wretched,

That sucked the honey of his musicked vows,

Now see that noble and most sovereign reason

Like sweet bells jangled, out of time and harsh,

That unmatched form and feature of blown youth

Blasted with ecstasy. O, woe is me

T' have seen what I have seen, see what I see!

[Enter King and Polonius]

King. Love? His affections do not that way tend,

Nor what he spake, though it lacked form a little,

Was not like madness. There's something in his soul

O'er which his melancholy sits on brood,

And I do doubt the hatch and the disclose

Will be some danger; which for to prevent,

I have in quick determination

Thus set it down: he shall with speed to England

For the demand of our neglected tribute.

Haply the seas, and countries different,
With variable objects, shall expel
This something-settled matter in his heart,
Whereon his brains still beating puts him thus
From fashion of himself. What think you on't?

Polonius. It shall do well. But yet do I believe
The origin and commencement of his grief
Sprung from neglected love. How now, Ophelia?
You need not tell us what Lord Hamlet said;
We heard it all. My lord, do as you please,
But if you hold it fit, after the play,
Let his queen mother all alone entreat him
To show his grief. Let her be round with him,
And I'll be placed, so please you, in the ear
Of all their conference. If she find him not,
To England send him, or confine him where
Your wisdom best shall think.

King.   It shall be so.
Madness in great ones must not unwatched go.
    [Exeunt]

SCENE II

WITHIN THE CASTLE

[Enter Hamlet and three of the Players]

Hamlet. Speak the speech, I pray you, as I pronounced it to you, trippingly on the tongue. But if you mouth it, as many of our players do, I had as lief the town crier spoke my lines. Nor do not saw the air too much with your hand, thus, but use all gently, for in the very torrent, tempest, and (as I may say) whirlwind of your passion, you must acquire and beget a temperance that may give it smoothness. O, it offends me to the soul to hear a robustious periwig-pated fellow tear a passion to tatters, to very rags, to split the ears of the groundlings, who for the most part are capable of nothing but inexplicable dumb shows and noise. I would have such a fellow whipped for o'erdoing Termagant. It out-herods Herod. Pray you avoid it.

Player. I warrant your honor.

Hamlet. Be not too tame neither, but let your own discretion be your tutor. Suit the action to the word, the word to the action, with this special observance, that you o'erstep not the modesty of nature. For anything so o'erdone is from the purpose of playing, whose end, both at the first and now, was and is, to hold, as 'twere, the mirror up to nature; to show virtue her own feature, scorn her own image, and the very age and body of the time his form and pressure. Now, this overdone, or come tardy off, though it makes the unskillful laugh, cannot but make the judicious grieve, the censure of the which one must in your allowance o'erweigh a whole theater of others. O, there be players that I have seen play, and heard others praise, and that highly (not to speak it profanely), that neither having th' accent of Christians, nor the gait of Christian, pagan, nor man, have so strutted and bellowed that I have thought some of Nature's journeymen had made men, and not made them well, they imitated humanity so abominably.

Player. I hope we have reformed that indifferently with us, sir.

Hamlet. O, reform it altogether! And let those that play your clowns speak no more than is set down for them, for there be of them that will themselves laugh, to set on some quantity of barren spectators to laugh too, though in the meantime some necessary question of the play be then to be considered. That's villainous and shows a most pitiful ambition in the fool that uses it. Go make you ready.

[*Exeunt Players. Enter Polonius, Guildenstern, and Rosencrantz*]

How now, my lord? Will the King hear this piece of work?

Polonius. And the Queen too, and that presently.

Hamlet. Bid the players make haste.

[*Exit Polonius*]

Will you two help to hasten them?

Both. We will my lord.

[*Exeunt*]

Hamlet. What, ho, Horatio!

[Enter Horatio]

Horatio.   Here, sweet lord, at your service.

Hamlet.   Horatio, thou art e'en as just a man

As e'er my conversation coped withal.

Horatio.   O, my dear lord—

Hamlet.   Nay, do not think I flatter.

For what advancement may I hope from thee,

That no revenue hast but thy good spirits

To feed and clothe thee? Why should the poor be flattered?

No, let the candied tongue lick absurd pomp,

And crook the pregnant hinges of the knee

Where thrift may follow fawning. Dost thou hear?

Since my dear soul was mistress of her choice

And could of men distinguish her election,

S' hath sealed thee for herself, for thou hast been

As one, in suff'ring all, that suffers nothing,

A man that Fortune's buffets and rewards

Hast ta'en with equal thanks; and blest are those

Whose blood and judgment are so well commeddled

That they are not a pipe for Fortune's finger

To sound what stop she please. Give me that man
That is not passion's slave, and I will wear him
In my heart's core, ay, in my heart of heart,
As I do thee. Something too much of this—
There is a play tonight before the King.
One scene of it comes near the circumstance
Which I have told thee, of my father's death.
I prithee, when thou seest that act afoot,
Even with the very comment of thy soul
Observe my uncle. If his occulted guilt
Do not itself unkennel in one speech,
It is a damnèd ghost that we have seen,
And my imaginations are as foul
As Vulcan's stithy. Give him heedful note,
For I mine eyes will rivet to his face,
And after we will both our judgments join
In censure of his seeming.

Horatio.   Well, my lord.
If 'a steal aught the whilst this play is playing,
And scape detecting, I will pay the theft.

[Enter King, Queen, Polonius, Ophelia, Rosencrantz, Guildenstern, and other Lords attendant with his Guards, carrying torches. Danish March. A flourish]

Hamlet. They are coming to the play: I must be idle;
Get you a place.

King. How fares our cousin Hamlet?

Hamlet. Excellent, i' faith, of the chameleon's dish; I
eat the air, promise-crammed; you cannot feed
capons so.

King. I have nothing with this answer, Hamlet; these
words are not mine.

Hamlet. No, nor mine now. *[To Polonius]* My lord, you
played once i' th' university, you say?

Polonius. That did I, my lord, and was accounted a good
actor.

Hamlet. What did you enact?

Polonius. I did enact Julius Caesar. I was killed i' th' Capitol; Brutus killed me.

Hamlet. It was a brute part of him to kill so capital a calf
there. Be the players ready?

Rosencrantz.	Ay, my lord. They stay upon your patience.
Queen.	Come hither, my dear Hamlet, sit by me.
Hamlet.	No, good mother. Here's metal more attractive.
Polonius.	[*To the King*] O ho! Do you mark that?
Hamlet.	Lady, shall I lie in your lap?

[*He lies at Ophelia's feet*]

Ophelia.	No, my lord.
Hamlet.	I mean, my head upon your lap?
Ophelia.	Ay, my lord.
Hamlet.	Do you think I meant country matters?
Ophelia.	I think nothing, my lord.
Hamlet.	That's a fair thought to lie between maids' legs.
Ophelia.	What is, my lord?
Hamlet.	Nothing.
Ophelia.	You are merry, my lord.
Hamlet.	Who, I?
Ophelia.	Ay, my lord.
Hamlet.	O God, your only jig-maker! What should a man do but be merry? For look you how cheerfully my mother looks, and my father died within's two hours.
Ophelia.	Nay, 'tis twice two months, my lord.

Hamlet. So long? Nay then, let the devil wear black, for I'll have a suit of sables. O heavens! Die two months ago, and not forgotten yet? Then there's hope a great man's memory may outlive his life half a year. But, by'r Lady, 'a must build churches then, or else shall 'a suffer not thinking on, with the hobbyhorse, whose epitaph is "For O, for O, the hobbyhorse is forgot!"

[*The trumpets sound. A dumb show follows: Enter a King and a Queen very lovingly, the Queen embracing him, and he her. She kneels; and makes show of protestation unto him. He takes her up, and declines his head upon her neck. He lies him down upon a bank of flowers. She, seeing him asleep, leaves him. Anon come in another man: takes off his crown, kisses it, pours poison in the sleeper's ears, and leaves him. The Queen returns, finds the King dead, makes passionate action. The poisoner, with some three or four, come in again, seem to lament with her. The dead body is carried away. The poisoner woos the Queen with gifts; she seems harsh awhile, but in the end accepts love*]
[*Exeunt*]

Ophelia.	What means this, my lord?
Hamlet.	Marry, this is miching mallecho; it means mis-chief.
Ophelia.	Belike this show imports the argument of the play.

[Enter Prologue]

Hamlet.	We shall know by this fellow. The players can-not keep counsel; they'll tell all.
Ophelia.	Will 'a tell us what this show meant?
Hamlet.	Ay, or any show that you will show him. Be not you ashamed to show, he'll not shame to tell you what it means.
Ophelia.	You are naught, you are naught; I'll mark the play.
Prologue.	For us, and for our tragedy,
	Here stooping to your clemency,
	We beg your hearing patiently.

[Exit]

Hamlet.	Is this a prologue, or the posy of a ring?
Ophelia.	'Tis brief, my lord.
Hamlet.	As woman's love.

Player King.   Full thirty times hath Phoebus' cart gone round

Neptune's salt wash and Tellus' orbèd ground,

And thirty dozen moons with borrowed sheen

About the world have times twelve thirties been,

Since love our hearts, and Hymen did our hands,

Unite commutual in most sacred bands.

Player Queen.   So many journeys may the sun and moon

Make us again count o'er ere love be done!

But woe is me, you are so sick of late,

So far from cheer and from your former state,

That I distrust you. Yet, though I distrust,

Discomfort you, my lord, it nothing must.

For women fear too much, even as they love,

And women's fear and love hold quantity,

In neither aught, or in extremity.

Now what my love is, proof hath made you know,

And as my love is sized, my fear is so.

Where love is great, the littlest doubts are fear;

Where little fears grow great, great love grows there.

Player King.	Faith, I must leave thee, love, and shortly too;
	My operant powers their functions leave to do:
	And thou shalt live in this fair world behind,
	Honored, beloved, and haply one as kind
	For husband shalt thou—
Player Queen.	O, confound the rest!
	Such love must needs be treason in my breast.
	In second husband let me be accurst!
	None wed the second but who killed the first.
Hamlet.	[*Aside*] Wormwood, wormwood.
Player Queen.	The instances that second marriage move
	Are base respects of thrift, but none of love.
	A second time I kill my husband dead
	When second husband kisses me in bed.
Player King.	I do believe you think what now you speak,
	But what we do determine oft we break.
	Purpose is but the slave to memory,
	Of violent birth, but poor validity,
	Which now like fruit unripe sticks on the tree,
	But fall unshaken when they mellow be.
	Most necessary 'tis that we forget
	To pay ourselves what to ourselves is debt.

What to ourselves in passion we propose,

The passion ending, doth the purpose lose.

The violence of either grief or joy

Their own enactures with themselves destroy:

Where joy most revels, grief doth most lament;

Grief joys, joy grieves, on slender accident.

This world is not for aye, nor 'tis not strange

That even our loves should with our fortunes change,

For 'tis a question left us yet to prove,

Whether love lead fortune, or else fortune love.

The great man down, you mark his favorite flies;

The poor advanced makes friends of enemies;

And hitherto doth love on fortune tend,

For who not needs shall never lack a friend;

And who in want a hollow friend doth try,

Directly seasons him his enemy.

But, orderly to end where I begun,

Our wills and fates do so contrary run

That our devices still are overthrown;

Our thoughts are ours, their ends none of our own.

So think thou wilt no second husband wed,

But die thy thoughts when thy first lord is dead.

Player Queen.	Nor earth to me give food, nor heaven light,
	Sport and repose lock from me day and night,
	To desperation turn my trust and hope,
	An anchor's cheer in prison be my scope,
	Each opposite that blanks the face of joy
	Meet what I would have well, and it destroy:
	Both here and hence pursue me lasting strife,
	If, once a widow, ever I be wife!
Hamlet.	If she should break it now!
Player King.	'Tis deeply sworn. Sweet, leave me here awhile;
	My spirits grow dull, and fain I would beguile
	The tedious day with sleep.
Player Queen.	Sleep rock thy brain,
	{*He sleeps*}
	And never come mischance between us twain!
	{*Exit*}
Hamlet.	Madam, how like you this play?
Queen.	The lady doth protest too much, methinks.
Hamlet.	O, but she'll keep her word.
King.	Have you heard the argument? Is there no offense in't?

Hamlet.	No, no, they do but jest, poison in jest; no offense i' th' world.
King.	What do you call the play?
Hamlet.	The Mousetrap. Marry, how? Tropically. This play is the image of a murder done in Vienna: Gonzago is the Duke's name; his wife, Baptista. You shall see anon. 'Tis a knavish piece of work, but what of that? Your Majesty, and we that have free souls, it touches us not. Let the galled jade winch; our withers are unwrung.

[Enter Lucianus]

	This is one Lucianus, nephew to the King.
Ophelia.	You are as good as a chorus, my lord.
Hamlet.	I could interpret between you and your love, if I could see the puppets dallying.
Ophelia.	You are keen, my lord, you are keen.
Hamlet.	It would cost you a groaning to take off mine edge.
Ophelia.	Still better, and worse.

Hamlet.	So you mistake your husbands.—Begin, murderer. Leave thy damnable faces and begin. Come, the croaking raven doth bellow for revenge.
Lucianus.	Thoughts black, hands apt, drugs fit, and time agreeing, Confederate season, else no creature seeing, Thou mixture rank, of midnight weeds collected, With Hecate's ban thrice blasted, thrice infected, Thy natural magic and dire property On wholesome life usurps immediately.

{*Pours the poison in his ears*}

Hamlet.	'A poisons him i' th' garden for his estate. His name's Gonzago. The story is extant, and written in very choice Italian. You shall see anon how the murderer gets the love of Gonzago's wife.
Ophelia.	The King rises.
Hamlet.	What, frighted with false fire?
Queen.	How fares my lord?
Polonius.	Give o'er the play.
King.	Give me some light. Away!
Polonius.	Lights, lights, lights!

{*Exeunt all but Hamlet and Horatio*}

Hamlet. Why, let the strucken deer go weep,
The hart ungallèd play:
For some must watch, while some must sleep;
Thus runs the world away.
Would not this, sir, and a forest of feathers—if
the rest of my fortunes turn Turk with me—with
two Provincial roses on my razed shoes, get me
a fellowship in a cry of players?

Horatio. Half a share.

Hamlet. A whole one, I.
For thou dost know, O Damon dear,
This realm dismantled was
Of Jove himself; and now reigns here
A very, very—pajock.

Horatio. You might have rhymed.

Hamlet. O good Horatio, I'll take the ghost's word for a
thousand pound. Didst perceive?

Horatio. Very well, my lord.

Hamlet. Upon the talk of poisoning?

Horatio. I did very well note him.

Hamlet.	Ah ha! Come, some music! Come, the recorders!
	For if the King like not the comedy,
	Why then, belike he likes it not, perdy.
	Come, some music!
	[*Enter Rosencrantz and Guildenstern*]
Guildenstern.	Good my lord, vouchsafe me a word with you.
Hamlet.	Sir, a whole history.
Guildenstern.	The King, sir—
Hamlet.	Ay, sir, what of him?
Guildenstern.	Is in his retirement marvelous distemp'red.
Hamlet.	With drink, sir?
Guildenstern.	No, my lord, with choler.
Hamlet.	Your wisdom should show itself more richer to signify this to the doctor, for for me to put him to his purgation would perhaps plunge him into more choler.
Guildenstern.	Good my lord, put your discourse into some frame, and start not so wildly from my affair.
Hamlet.	I am tame, sir; pronounce.

Guildenstern. The Queen, your mother, in most great affliction of spirit hath sent me to you.

Hamlet. You are welcome.

Guildenstern. Nay, good my lord, this courtesy is not of the
right breed. If it shall please you to make me a
wholesome answer, I will do your mother's commandment; if not, your pardon and my return
shall be the end of my business.

Hamlet. Sir, I cannot.

Rosencrantz. What, my lord?

Hamlet. Make you a wholesome answer; my wit's dis-
eased. But, sir, such answer as I can make, you
shall command, or rather, as you say, my
mother. Therefore no more, but to the matter.
My mother, you say—

Rosencrantz. Then thus she says: your behavior hath struck
her into amazement and admiration.

Hamlet. O wonderful son, that can so stonish a mother!
But is there no sequel at the heels of this
mother's admiration? Impart.

Rosencrantz.	She desires to speak with you in her closet ere you go to bed.
Hamlet.	We shall obey, were she ten times our mother. Have you any further trade with us?
Rosencrantz.	My lord, you once did love me.
Hamlet.	And do still, by these pickers and stealers.
Rosencrantz.	Good my lord, what is your cause of distemper? You do surely bar the door upon your own liberty, if you deny your griefs to your friend.
Hamlet.	Sir, I lack advancement.
Rosencrantz.	How can that be, when you have the voice of the King himself for your succession in Denmark?

[*Enter the Players with recorders*]

Hamlet.	Ay, sir, but "while the grass grows"—the proverb is something musty. O, the recorders. Let me see one. To withdraw with you—why do you go about to recover the wind of me as if you would drive me into a toil?
Guildenstern.	O my lord, if my duty be too bold, my love is too unmannerly.

Hamlet.	I do not well understand that. Will you play upon this pipe?
Guildenstern.	My lord, I cannot.
Hamlet.	I pray you.
Guildenstern.	Believe me, I cannot.
Hamlet.	I pray you.
Guildenstern.	Believe me, I cannot.
Hamlet.	I do beseech you.
Guildenstern.	I know no touch of it, my lord.
Hamlet.	It is as easy as lying. Govern these ventages with your fingers and thumb, give it breath with your mouth, and it will discourse most eloquent music. Look you, these are the stops.
Guildenstern.	But these cannot I command to any utt'rance of harmony; I have not the skill.
Hamlet.	Why, look you now, how unworthy a thing you make of me! You would play upon me; you woud seem to know my stops; you would pluck out the heart of my mystery; you would sound me from my lowest note to the top of my compass; and there is much music, excellent voice,

in this little organ, yet cannot you make it speak. 'Sblood, do you think I am easier to be played on than a pipe? Call me what instrument you will, though you can fret me, you cannot play upon me.

[*Enter Polonius*]

God bless you, sir!

Polonius. My lord, the Queen would speak with you, and presently.

Hamlet. Do you see yonder cloud that's almost in shape of a camel?

Polonius. By th' mass and 'tis, like a camel indeed.

Hamlet. Methinks it is like a weasel.

Polonius. It is backed like a weasel.

Hamlet. Or like a whale.

Polonius. Very like a whale.

Hamlet. Then I will come to my mother by and by.

[*Aside*] They fool me to the top of my bent.—I will come by and by.

Polonius.   I will say so.

          {Exit}

Hamlet. "By and by" is easily said. Leave me, friends.

          {Exeunt all but Hamlet}

'Tis now the very witching time of night,

When churchyards yawn, and hell itself breathes out

Contagion to this world. Now could I drink hot blood

And do such bitter business as the day

Would quake to look on. Soft, now to my mother.

O heart, lose not thy nature; let not ever

The soul of Nero enter this firm bosom.

Let me be cruel, not unnatural;

I will speak daggers to her, but use none.

My tongue and soul in this be hypocrites:

How in my words somever she be shent,

To give them seals never, my soul, consent!

          {Exit}

SCENE III

WITHIN THE CASTLE

[Enter King, Rosencrantz, and Guildenstern]

King. I like him not, nor stands it safe with us
To let his madness range. Therefore prepare you.
I your commission will forthwith dispatch,
And he to England shall along with you.
The terms of our estate may not endure
Hazard so near's as doth hourly grow
Out of his brows.

Guildenstern. We will ourselves provide.
Most holy and religious fear it is
To keep those many many bodies safe
That live and feed upon your Majesty.

Rosencrantz.   The single and peculiar life is bound

With all the strength and armor of the mind

To keep itself from noyance, but much more

The spirit upon whose weal depends and rests

The lives of many. The cess of majesty

Dies not alone, but like a gulf doth draw

What's near it with it; or it is a massy wheel

Fixed on the summit of the highest mount,

To whose huge spokes ten thousand lesser things

Are mortised and adjoined, which when it falls,

Each small annexment, petty consequence,

Attends the boist'rous ruin. Never alone

Did the King sigh, but with a general groan.

King.   Arm you, I pray you, to this speedy voyage,

For we will fetters put about this fear,

Which now goes too free-footed.

Rosencrantz.   We will haste us.

{*Exeunt Gentlemen. Enter Polonius*}

Polonius.　My lord, he's going to his mother's closet.

Behind the arras I'll convey myself

To hear the process. I'll warrant she'll tax him home,

And, as you said, and wisely was it said,

'Tis meet that some more audience than a mother,

Since nature makes them partial, should o'erhear

The speech of vantage. Fare you well, my liege.

I'll call upon you ere you go to bed

And tell you what I know.

King.　　　　　　　　　　　Thanks, dear my lord.

[Exit Polonius]

O, my offense is rank, it smells to heaven;

It hath the primal eldest curse upon't,

A brother's murder. Pray can I not,

Though inclination be as sharp as will.

My stronger guilt defeats my strong intent,

And like a man to double business bound

I stand in pause where I shall first begin,

And both neglect. What if this cursèd hand
Were thicker than itself with brother's blood,
Is there not rain enough in the sweet heavens
To wash it white as snow? Whereto serves mercy
But to confront the visage of offense?
And what's in prayer but this twofold force,
To be forestallèd ere we come to fall,
Or pardoned being down? Then I'll look up.
My fault is past. But, O, what form of prayer
Can serve my turn? "Forgive me my foul murder"?
That cannot be, since I am still possessed
Of those effects for which I did the murder,
My crown, mine own ambition, and my queen.
May one be pardoned and retain th' offense?
In the corrupted currents of this world
Offense's gilded hand may shove by justice,
And oft 'tis seen the wicked prize itself
Buys out the law. But 'tis not so above.
There is no shuffling; there the action lies
In his true nature, and we ourselves compelled,

Even to the teeth and forehead of our faults,
To give in evidence. What then? What rests?
Try what repentance can. What can it not?
Yet what can it when one cannot repent?
O wretched state! O bosom black as death!
O limèd soul, that struggling to be free
Art more engaged! Help, angels! Make assay.
Bow, stubborn knees, and, heart with strings of steel,
Be soft as sinews of the newborn babe.
All may be well. [*He kneels*]
    [*Enter Hamlet*]

Hamlet. Now might I do it pat, now 'a is a-praying,
And now I'll do't. And so 'a goes to heaven,
And so am I revenged. That would be scanned.
A villain kills my father, and for that
I, his sole son, do this same villain send
To heaven.
Why, this is hire and salary, not revenge.
'A took my father grossly, full of bread,

With all his crimes broad blown, as flush as May;
And how his audit stands, who knows save heaven?
But in our circumstance and course of thought,
'Tis heavy with him; and am I then revenged,
To take him in the purging of his soul,
When he is fit and seasoned for his passage?
No.
Up, sword, and know thou a more horrid hent.
When he is drunk asleep, or in his rage,
Or in th' incestuous pleasure of his bed,
At game a-swearing, or about some act
That has no relish of salvation in't—
Then trip him, that his heels may kick at heaven,
And that his soul may be as damned and black
As hell, whereto it goes. My mother stays.
This physic but prolongs thy sickly days.
　　　　[Exit]

King.　　*[Rises]* My words fly up, my thought s remain below.
　　Words without thoughts never to heaven go.
　　　　[Exit]

SCENE IV

THE QUEEN'S CLOSET

[*Enter Queen Gertrude and Polonius*]

Polonius. 'A will come straight. Look you lay home to him.
Tell him his pranks have been too broad to bear with,
And that your Grace hath screened and stood between
Much heat and him. I'll silence me even here.
Pray you be round with him.

Hamlet. [*Within*] Mother, Mother, Mother!

Queen. I'll warrant you; fear me not. Withdraw; I hear him
coming.

[*Polonius hides behind the curtain. Enter Hamlet*]

Hamlet. Now, Mother, what's the matter?

Queen. Hamlet, thou hast thy father much offended.

Hamlet. Mother, you have my father much offended.

Queen. Come, come, you answer with an idle tongue.

Hamlet. Go, go, you question with a wicked tongue.

Queen. Why, how now, Hamlet?

Hamlet.   What's the matter now?

Queen.	Have you forgot me?
Hamlet.	No, by the rood, not so!
	You are the Queen, your husband's brother's wife,
	And, would it were not so, you are my mother.
Queen.	Nay, then I'll set those to you that can speak.
Hamlet.	Come, come, and sit you down. You shall not budge.
	You go not till I set you up a glass
	Where you may see the inmost part of you!
Queen.	What wilt thou do? Thou wilt not murder me?
	Help, ho!
Polonius.	[*Behind*] What, ho! Help!
Hamlet.	[*Draws*] How now? A rat? Dead for a ducat, dead!
	[*Makes a pass through the curtain and kills Polonius*]
Polonius.	[*Behind*] O, I am slain!
Queen.	O me, what hast thou done?
Hamlet.	Nay, I know not. Is it the king?
Queen.	O, what a rash and bloody deed is this!
Hamlet.	A bloody deed—almost as bad, good Mother,
	As kill a king, and marry with his brother.

Queen.	As kill a king?
Hamlet.	Ay, lady, it was my word.

{Lifts up the curtain and sees Polonius}

Thou wretched, rash, intruding fool, farewell!
I took thee for thy better. Take thy fortune.
Thou find'st to be too busy is some danger.—
Leave wringing of your hands. Peace, sit you down
And let me wring your heart, for so I shall
If it be made of penetrable stuff,
If damnèd custom have not brazed it so
That it be proof and bulwark against sense.

Queen.	What have I done that thou dar'st wag thy tongue
	In noise so rude against me?
Hamlet.	Such an act

That blurs the grace and blush of modesty,
Calls virtue hypocrite, takes off the rose
From the fair forehead of an innocent love,
And sets a blister there, makes marriage vows
As false as dicers' oaths. O, such a deed
As from the body of contraction plucks

The very soul, and sweet religion makes
A rhapsody of words! Heaven's face does glow
O'er this solidity and compound mass
With heated visage, as against the doom
Is thoughtsick at the act.

Queen.   Ay me, what act,
That roars so loud and thunders in the index?

Hamlet.   Look here upon this picture, and on this,
The counterfeit presentment of two brothers.
See what a grace was seated on this brow:
Hyperion's curls, the front of Jove himself,
An eye like Mars, to threaten and command,
A station like the herald Mercury
New lighted on a heaven-kissing hill—
A combination and a form indeed
Where every god did seem to set his seal
To give the world assurance of a man.
This was your husband. Look you now what follows.
Here is your husband, like a mildewed ear
Blasting his wholesome brother. Have you eyes?
Could you on this fair mountain leave to feed,

And batten on this moor? Ha! Have you eyes?
You cannot call it love, for at your age
The heyday in the blood is tame, it's humble,
And waits upon the judgment, and what judgment
Would step from this to this? Sense sure you have,
Else could you not have motion, but sure that sense
Is apoplexed, for madness would not err,
Nor sense to ecstasy was ne'er so thralled
But it reserved some quantity of choice
To serve in such a difference. What devil was't
That thus hath cozened you at hoodman-blind?
Eyes without feeling, feeling without sight,
Ears without hands or eyes, smelling sans all,
Or but a sickly part of one true sense
Could not so mope.
O shame, where is thy blush? Rebellious hell,
If thou canst mutine in a matron's bones,
To flaming youth let virtue be as wax
And melt in her own fire. Proclaim no shame
When the compulsive ardor gives the charge,
Since frost itself as actively doth burn,
And reason panders will.

Queen.   O Hamlet, speak no more.
Thou turn'st mine eyes into my very soul,
And there I see such black and grainèd spots
As will not leave their tinct.

Hamlet.   Nay, but to live
In the rank sweat of an enseamèd bed,
Stewed in corruption, honeying and making love
Over the nasty sty—

Queen.   O, speak to me no more.
These words like daggers enter in my ears.
No more, sweet Hamlet.

Hamlet.   A murderer and a villain,
A slave that is not twentieth part the tithe
Of your precedent lord, a vice of kings,
A cutpurse of the empire and the rule,
That from a shelf the precious diadem stole
And put it in his pocket—

Queen.   No more.

                    [Enter Ghost]

Hamlet. A king of shreds and patches—
Save me and hover o'er me with your wings,
You heavenly guards! What would your gracious figure?

Queen.	Alas, he's mad.
Hamlet.	Do you not come your tardy son to chide,
	That, lapsed in time and passion, lets go by
	Th' important acting of your dread command?
	O, say!
Ghost.	Do not forget. This visitation
	Is but to whet thy almost blunted purpose.
	But look, amazement on thy mother sits.
	O, step between her and her fighting soul!
	Conceit in weakest bodies strongest works.
	Speak to her, Hamlet.
Hamlet.	How is it with you, lady?
Queen.	Alas, how is't with you,
	That you do bend your eye on vacancy,
	And with th' incorporal air do hold discourse?
	Forth at your eyes your spirits wildly peep,
	And as the sleeping soldiers in th' alarm
	Your bedded hair like life in excrements
	Start up and stand an end. O gentle son,
	Upon the heat and flame of thy distemper
	Sprinkle cool patience. Whereon do you look?

Hamlet.	On him, on him! Look you, how pale he glares!
	His form and cause conjoined, preaching to stones,
	Would make them capable.—Do not look upon me,
	Lest with this piteous action you convert
	My stern effects. Then what I have to do
	Will want true color; tears perchance for blood.
Queen.	To whom do you speak this?
Hamlet.	Do you see nothing there?
Queen.	Nothing at all; yet all that is I see.
Hamlet.	Nor did you nothing hear?
Queen.	No, nothing but ourselves.
Hamlet.	Why, look you there! Look how it steals away!
	My father, in his habit as he lived!
	Look where he goes even now out at the portal!
	{*Exit Ghost*}
Queen.	This is the very coinage of your brain.
	This bodiless creation ecstasy is very cunning in.

Hamlet. Ecstasy?
My pulse as yours doth temperately keep time
And makes as healthful music. It is not madness
That I have uttered. Bring me to the test,
And I the matter will reword, which madness
Would gambol from. Mother, for love of grace,
Lay not that flattering unction to your soul,
That not your trespass but my madness speaks.
It will but skin and film the ulcerous place
Whiles rank corruption, mining all within,
Infects unseen. Confess yourself to heaven,
Repent what's past, avoid what is to come,
And do not spread the compost on the weeds
To make them ranker. Forgive me this my virtue.
For in the fatness of these pursy times
Virtue itself of vice must pardon beg,
Yea, curb and woo for leave to do him good.
Queen. O Hamlet,
Thou hast cleft my heart in twain.

Hamlet.   O, throw away the worser part of it,
And live the purer with the other half.
Good night—but go not to my uncle's bed.
Assume a virtue, if you have it not.
That monster custom, who all sense doth eat,
Of habits devil, is angel yet in this,
That to the use of actions fair and good
He likewise gives a frock or livery
That aptly is put on. Refrain tonight,
And that shall lend a kind of easiness
To the next abstinence; the next more easy;
For use almost can change the stamp of nature,
And either the devil, or throw him out
With wondrous potency. Once more, good night,
And when you are desirous to be blest,
I'll blessing beg of you.—For this same lord,
I do repent; but heaven hath pleased it so,
To punish me with this, and this with me,
That I must be their scourge and minister.
I will bestow him and will answer well
The death I gave him. So again, good night.

I must be cruel only to be kind.

Thus bad begins, and worse remains behind.

One word more, good lady.

Queen. What shall I do?

Hamlet. Not this, by no means, that I bid you do:

Let the bloat King tempt you again to bed,

Pinch wanton on your cheek, call you his mouse,

And let him, for a pair of reechy kisses,

Or paddling in your neck with his damned fingers,

Make you to ravel all this matter out,

That I essentially am not in madness,

But mad in craft. 'Twere good you let him know,

For who that's but a queen, fair, sober, wise,

Would from a paddock, from a bat, a gib,

Such dear concernings hide? Who would do so?

No, in despite of sense and secrecy,

Unpeg the basket on the house's top,

Let the birds fly, and like the famous ape,

To try conclusions, in the basket creep

And break your own neck down.

Queen.	Be thou assured, if words be made of breath,
	And breath of life, I have no life to breathe
	What thou hast said to me.
Hamlet.	I must to England; you know that?
Queen.	Alack,
	I had forgot. 'Tis so concluded on.
Hamlet.	There's letters sealed, and my two schoolfellows,
	Whom I will trust as I will adders fanged,
	They bear the mandate; they must sweep my way
	And marshal me to knavery. Let it work;
	For 'tis the sport to have the enginer
	Hoist with his own petar, and 't shall go hard
	But I will delve one yard below their mines
	And blow them at the moon. O, 'tis most sweet
	When in one line two crafts directly meet.
	This man shall set me packing:
	I'll lug the guts into the neighbor room.
	Mother, good night. Indeed, this counselor
	Is now most still, most secret, and most grave,
	Who was in life a foolish prating knave.
	Come, sir, to draw toward an end with you.
	Good night, Mother.

       {Exit the Queen, then Hamlet, tugging Polonius}

ACT FOUR

SCENE I

WITHIN THE CASTLE

[Enter the King and Queen, with
Rosencrantz and Guildenstern]

King. There's matter in these sighs. These profound heaves
You must translate; 'tis fit we understand them.
Where is your son?

Queen. Bestow this place on us a little while.
[Exeunt Rosencrantz and Guildenstern]
Ah, mine own lord, what have I seen tonight!

King. What, Gertrude? How does Hamlet?

Queen. Mad as the sea and wind when both contend
Which is the mightier. In his lawless fit,
Behind the arras hearing something stir,
Whips out his rapier, cries, "A rat, a rat!"
And in this brainish apprehension kills
The unseen good old man.

King.   O heavy deed!
It had been so with us, had we been there.
His liberty is full of threats to all,
To you yourself, to us, to every one.
Alas, how shall this bloody deed be answered?
It will be laid to us, whose providence
Should have kept short, restrained, and out of haunt
This mad young man. But so much was our love
We would not understand what was most fit,
But, like the owner of a foul disease,
To keep it from divulging, let it feed
Even on the pith of life. Where is he gone?
Queen. To draw apart the body he hath killed;
O'er whom his very madness, like some ore
Among a mineral of metals base,
Shows itself pure. 'A weeps for what is done.

King. O Gertrude, come away!
The sun no sooner shall the mountains touch
But we will ship him hence, and this vile deed
We must with all our majesty and skill
Both countenance and excuse. Ho, Guildenstern!

{*Enter Rosencrantz and Guildenstern*}

Friends both, go join you with some further aid:
Hamlet in madness hath Polonius slain,
And from his mother's closet hath he dragged him.
Go seek him out; speak fair, and bring the body
Into the chapel. I pray you haste in this.

{*Exeunt Rosencrantz and Guildenstern*}

Come, Gertrude, we'll call up our wisest friends
And let them know both what we mean to do
And what's untimely done . . .
Whose whisper o'er the world's diameter,
As level as the cannon to his blank
Transports his poisoned shot, may miss our name
And hit the woundless air. O, come away!
My soul is full of discord and dismay.

{*Exeunt*}

[Enter Hamlet]

Hamlet.   Safely stowed.

Gentlemen.   *[Within]* Hamlet! Lord Hamlet!

Hamlet.   But soft, what noise? Who calls on Hamlet?
    O, here they come.

[Enter Rosencrantz and Guildenstern]

Rosencrantz.   What have you done, my lord, with the dead body?

Hamlet.   Compounded it with dust, whereto 'tis kin.

Rosencrantz.   Tell us where 'tis, that we may take it thence
    And bear it to the chapel.

Hamlet.   Do not believe it.

Rosencrantz.   Believe what?

Hamlet.   That I can keep your counsel and not mine own.
    Besides, to be demanded of a sponge, what rep-
    lication should be made by the son of a king?

Rosencrantz.   Take you me for a sponge, my lord?

Hamlet. Ay, sir, that soaks up the King's countenance, his rewards, his authorities. But such officers do the King best service in the end. He keeps them, like an ape, in the corner of his jaw, first mouthed, to be last swallowed. When he needs what you have gleaned, it is but squeezing you and, sponge, you shall be dry again.

Rosencrantz. I understand you not, my lord.

Hamlet. I am glad of it: a knavish speech sleeps in a foolish ear.

Rosencrantz. My lord, you must tell us where the body is and go with us to the King.

Hamlet. The body is with the King, but the King is not with the body. The King is a thing—

Guildenstern. A thing, my lord?

Hamlet. Of nothing. Bring me to him. Hide fox, and all after.

{*Exeunt*}

SCENE III

WITHIN THE CASTLE

[Enter King, and two or three]

King. I have sent to seek him and to find the body:
How dangerous is it that this man goes loose!
Yet must not we put the strong law on him:
He's loved of the distracted multitude,
Who like not in their judgment, but their eyes,
And where 'tis so, th' offender's scourge is weighed,
But never the offense. To bear all smooth and even,
This sudden sending him away must seem
Deliberate pause. Diseases desperate grown
By desperate appliance are relieved,
Or not at all.

[Enter Rosencrantz, Guildenstern, and others]

                 How now? What hath befall'n?

Rosencrantz. Where the dead body is bestowed, my lord,
We cannot get from him.

King.   But where is he?

Rosencrantz. Without, my lord; guarded, to know your pleasure.

King.	Bring him before us.
Rosencrantz.	Ho! Bring in the lord.

[*They enter*]

King.	Now, Hamlet, where's Polonius?
Hamlet.	At supper.
King.	At supper? Where?
Hamlet.	Not where he eats, but where 'a is eaten. A certain convocation of politic worms are e'en at him. Your worm is your only emperor for diet. We fat all creatures else to fat us, and we fat ourselves for maggots. Your fat king and your lean beggar is but variable service—two dishes, but to one table. That's the end.
King.	Alas, alas!
Hamlet.	A man may fish with the worm that hath eat of a king, and eat of the fish that hath fed of that worm.
King.	What dost thou mean by this?
Hamlet.	Nothing but to show you how a king may go a progress through the guts of a beggar.
King.	Where is Polonius?

Hamlet.　In heaven. Send thither to see. If your messenger find him not there, seek him i' th' other
place yourself. But if indeed you find him not
within this month, you shall nose him as you go
up the stairs into the lobby.

King.　[*To Attendants*] Go seek him there.

Hamlet.　'A will stay till you come.

　　　　　　　[*Exeunt Attendants*]

King.　Hamlet, this deed, for thine especial safety,
Which we do tender as we dearly grieve
For that which thou hast done, must send thee hence
With fiery quickness. Therefore prepare thyself.
The bark is ready and the wind at help,
Th' associates tend, and everything is bent
For England.

Hamlet.　　　　　For England?

King.　　　　　　　　　Ay, Hamlet.

Hamlet.　　　　　　　　　　　Good.

King.　So is it, if thou knew'st our purposes.

Hamlet.　I see a cherub that sees them. But come, for
England! Farewell, dear Mother.

King. Thy loving father, Hamlet.

Hamlet. My mother—father and mother is man and wife,
man and wife is one flesh, and so, my mother.
Come, for England!
[Exit]

King. Follow him at foot; tempt him with speed aboard.
Delay it not; I'll have him hence tonight.
Away! For everything is sealed and done
That else leans on th' affair. Pray you make haste.
[Exeunt all but the King]
And, England, if my love thou hold'st at aught—
As my great power thereof may give thee sense,
Since yet thy cicatrice looks raw and red
After the Danish sword, and thy free awe
Pays homage to us—thou mayst not coldly set
Our sovereign process, which imports at full
By letters congruing to that effect
The present death of Hamlet. Do it, England,
For like the hectic in my blood he rages,
And thou must cure me. Till I know 'tis done,
Howe'er my haps, my joys were ne'er begun.
[Exit]

[Enter Fortinbras with an Army]

Fortinbras. Go, Captain, from me greet the Danish king.
Tell him that by his license Fortinbras
Craves the conveyance of a promised march
Over his kingdom. You know the rendezvous.
If that his Majesty would aught with us,
We shall express our duty in his eye;
And let him know so.

Captain.   I will do't, my lord.

Fortinbras. Go softly on.

*[Exeunt all but the Captain and
enter Hamlet, Rosencrantz, Etc]*

Hamlet. Good sir, whose powers are these?

Captain. They are of Norway, sir.

Hamlet. How purposed, sir, I pray you?

Captain. Against some part of Poland.

Hamlet.	Who commands them, sir?
Captain.	The nephew to old Norway, Fortinbras.
Hamlet.	Goes it against the main of Poland, sir,
	Or for some frontier?
Captain.	Truly to speak, and with no addition,
	We go to gain a little patch of ground
	That hath in it no profit but the name.
	To pay five ducats, five, I would not farm it,
	Nor will it yield to Norway or the Pole
	A ranker rate, should it be sold in fee.
Hamlet.	Why, then the Polack never will defend it.
Captain.	Yes, it is already garrisoned.
Hamlet.	Two thousand souls and twenty thousand ducats
	Will not debate the question of this straw.
	This is th' imposthume of much wealth and peace,
	That inward breaks, and shows no cause without
	Why the man dies. I humbly thank you, sir.
Captain.	God bye you, sir.
	[*Exit*]
Rosencrantz.	Will't please you go, my lord?

Hamlet.   I'll be with you straight. Go a little before.
                [Exeunt all but Hamlet]
            How all occasions do inform against me
            And spur my dull revenge! What is a man,
            If his chief good and market of his time
            Be but to sleep and feed? A beast, no more.
            Sure he that made us with such large discourse,
            Looking before and after, gave us not
            That capability and godlike reason
            To fust in us unused. Now, whether it be
            Bestial oblivion, or some craven scruple
            Of thinking too precisely on th' event—
            A thought which, quartered, hath but one part wisdom
            And ever three parts coward—I do not know
            Why yet I live to say, "This thing's to do,"
            Sith I have cause, and will, and strength, and means
            To do't. Examples gross as earth exhort me.
            Witness this army of such mass and charge,
            Led by a delicate and tender prince,
            Whose spirit, with divine ambition puffed,

Makes mouths at the invisible event,
Exposing what is mortal and unsure
To all that fortune, death, and danger dare,
Even for an eggshell. Rightly to be great
Is not to stir without great argument,
But greatly to find quarrel in a straw
When honor's at the stake. How stand I then,
That have a father killed, a mother stained,
Excitements of my reason and my blood,
And let all sleep, while to my shame I see
The imminent death of twenty thousand men
That for a fantasy and trick of fame
Go to their graves like beds, fight for a plot
Whereon the numbers cannot try the cause,
Which is not tomb enough and continent
To hide the slain? O, from this time forth,
My thoughts be bloody, or be nothing worth!
    {*Exit*}

SCENE V

WITHIN THE CASTLE

[*Enter Horatio, Queen Gertrude, and a Gentleman*]

Queen.   I will not speak with her.

Gentleman.   She is importunate, indeed distract.
    Her mood will needs be pitied.

Queen.   What would she have?

Gentleman.   She speaks much of her father, says she hears
    There's tricks i' th' world, and hems, and beats her heart,
    Spurns enviously at straws, speaks things in doubt
    That carry but half sense. Her speech is nothing,
    Yet the unshapèd use of it doth move
    The hearers to collection; they yawn at it,
    And botch the words up fit to their own thoughts,
    Which, as her winks and nods and gestures yield them,
    Indeed would make one think there might be thought,
    Though nothing sure, yet much unhappily.

Horatio.   'Twere good she were spoken with, for she may strew
    Dangerous conjectures in ill-breeding minds.

Queen. Let her come in.

       [Exit Gentleman]

       [Aside] To my sick soul (as sin's true nature is)

       Each toy seems prologue to some great amiss;

       So full of artless jealousy is guilt

       It spills itself in fearing to be spilt.

       [Enter Ophelia distracted]

Ophelia. Where is the beauteous majesty of Denmark?

Queen. How now, Ophelia?

Ophelia. *[Sings]*   How should I your truelove know

              From another one?

              By his cockle hat and staff

              And his sandal shoon.

Queen. Alas, sweet lady, what imports this song?

Ophelia. Say you? Nay, pray you mark.

       [Sings]   He is dead and gone, lady,

               He is dead and gone;

              At his head a grass-green turf,

              At his heels a stone.

       O, ho!

Queen. Nay, but Ophelia—

Ophelia. Pray you mark.

    {Sings}   White his shroud as the mountain snow—

      {Enter King}

Queen. Alas, look here, my lord.

Ophelia. *{Sings}*   Larded all with sweet flowers
                    Which bewept to the grave did not go
                    With truelove showers.

King. How do you, pretty lady?

Ophelia. Well, God dild you! They say the owl was a baker's daughter. Lord, we know what we are, but know not what we may be. God be at your table!

King. Conceit upon her father.

Ophelia. Pray let's have no words of this, but when they ask you what it means, say you this:

    {Sings}   Tomorrow is Saint Valentine's day.
                  All in the morning betime,
                  And I a maid at your window,
                  To be your Valentine.
                  Then up he rose and donned his clothes
                  And dupped the chamber door,
                  Let in the maid, that out a maid
                  Never departed more.

King. Pretty Ophelia.

Ophelia. Indeed, la, without an oath, I'll make an end on't:

[*Sings*]   By Gis and by Saint Charity,
Alack, and fie for shame!
Young men will do't if they come to't,
By Cock, they are to blame.
Quoth she, "Before you tumbled me,
You promised me to wed."

He answers:

[*Sings*]   "So would I 'a' done, by yonder sun,
An thou hadst not come to my bed."

King. How long hath she been thus?

Ophelia. I hope all will be well. We must be patient, but I cannot choose but weep to think they would lay him i' th' cold ground. My brother shall know of it; and so I thank you for your good counsel. Come, my coach! Good night, ladies, good night. Sweet ladies, good night, good night.

[*Exit*]

King. Follow her close; give her good watch, I pray you.
      [*Exit Horatio*]
    O, this is the poison of deep grief; it springs
    All from her father's death—and now behold!
    O Gertrude, Gertrude,
    When sorrows come, they come not single spies,
    But in battalions: first, her father slain;
    Next, your son gone, and he most violent author
    Of his own just remove; the people muddied,
    Thick and unwholesome in their thoughts and whispers
    For good Polonius' death, and we have done but greenly
    In huggermugger to inter him; poor Ophelia
    Divided from herself and her fair judgment,
    Without the which we are pictures or mere beasts;
    Last, and as much containing as all these,
    Her brother is in secret come from France,
    Feeds on his wonder, keeps himself in clouds,
    And wants not buzzers to infect his ear
    With pestilent speeches of his father's death,
    Wherein necessity, of matter beggared,

Will nothing stick our person to arraign

In ear and ear. O my dear Gertrude, this,

Like to a murd'ring piece, in many places

Gives me superfluous death.

{A noise within. Enter a Messenger}

Queen.   Alack, what noise is this?

King.   Attend, where are my Switzers?

Let them guard the door.

What is the matter?

Messenger.   Save yourself, my lord.

The ocean, overpeering of his list,

Eats not the flats with more impiteous haste

Than young Laertes, in a riotous head,

O'erbears your officers. The rabble call him lord,

And, as the world were now but to begin,

Antiquity forgot, custom not known,

The ratifiers and props of every word,

They cry, "Choose we! Laertes shall be king!"

Caps, hands, and tongues applaud it to the clouds,

"Laertes shall be king! Laertes king!"

{A noise within}

Queen.	How cheerfully on the false trail they cry!
	O, this is counter, you false Danish dogs!
	[Enter Laertes with others]
King.	The doors are broke.
Laertes.	Where is this king?—Sirs, stand you all without.
All.	No, let's come in.
Laertes.	I pray you give me leave.
All.	We will, we will.
Laertes.	I thank you. Keep the door.
	[Exeunt his Followers]
	O thou vile King,
	Give me my father.
Queen.	Calmly, good Laertes.
Laertes.	That drop of blood that's calm proclaims me bastard,
	Cries cuckold to my father, brands the harlot
	Even here between the chaste unsmirchèd brow
	Of my true mother.

King.   What is the cause, Laertes,
          That thy rebellion looks so giantlike?
          Let him go, Gertrude. Do not fear our person.
          There's such divinity doth hedge a king
          That treason can but peep to what it would,
          Acts little of his will. Tell me, Laertes,
          Why thou art thus incensed. Let him go, Gertrude.
          Speak, man.
Laertes. Where is my father?
King.   Dead.
Queen.   But not by him.
King.   Let him demand his fill.
Laertes. How came he dead? I'll not be juggled with.
          To hell allegiance, vows to the blackest devil,
          Conscience and grace to the profoundest pit!
          I dare damnation. To this point I stand,
          That both the worlds I give to negligence,
          Let come what comes, only I'll be revenged
          Most thoroughly for my father.
King.   Who shall stay you?

Laertes.	My will, not all the world's.
	And for my means, I'll husband them so well
	They shall go far with little.
King.	Good Laertes,
	If you desire to know the certainty
	Of your dear father, is't writ in your revenge
	That swoopstake you will draw both friend and foe,
	Winner and loser?
Laertes.	None but his enemies.
King.	Will you know them then?
Laertes.	To his good friends thus wide I'll ope my arms
	And like the kind life-rend'ring pelican
	Repast them with my blood.
King.	Why, now you speak
	Like a good child and a true gentleman.
	That I am guiltless of your father's death,
	And am most sensibly in grief for it,
	It shall as level to your judgment 'pear
	As day does to your eye.

[A noise within: "Let her come in"]

Laertes.   How now? What noise is that?

                [*Enter Ophelia*]

        O heat, dry up my brains; tears seven times salt

        Burn out the sense and virtue of mine eye!

        By heaven, thy madness shall be paid with weight

        Till our scale turn the beam. O rose of May,

        Dear maid, kind sister, sweet Ophelia!

        O heavens, is't possible a young maid's wits

        Should be as mortal as an old man's life?

        Nature is fine in love, and where 'tis fine,

        It sends some precious instance of itself

        After the thing it loves.

Ophelia.   [*Sings*]   They bore him barefaced on the bier

                        Hey non nony, nony, hey nony

                        And in his grave rained many a tear—

        Fare you well, my dove!

Laertes.   Hadst thou thy wits, and didst persuade revenge,

        It could not move thus.

Ophelia. You must sing "A-down a-down, and you call him a-down-a." O, how the wheel becomes it! It is the false steward, that stole his master's daughter.

Laertes. This nothing's more than matter.

Ophelia. There's rosemary, that's for remembrance. Pray you, love, remember. And there is pansies, that's for thoughts.

Laertes. A document in madness, thoughts and remembrance fitted.

Ophelia. There's fennel for you, and columbines. There's rue for you, and here's some for me. We may call it herb of grace o' Sundays. O, you must wear your rue with a difference. There's a daisy. I would give you some violets, but they withered all when my father died. They say 'a made a good end.

[*Sings*]   For bonny sweet Robin is all my joy.

Laertes. Thought and affliction, passion, hell itself, She turns to favor and to prettiness.

Ophelia.	[*Sings*]	And will 'a not come again?
		And will 'a not come again?
		No, no, he is dead,
		Go to thy deathbed,
		He never will come again.
		His beard was as white as snow,
		All flaxen was his poll.
		He is gone, he is gone,
		And we cast away moan.
		God 'a' mercy on his soul!

And of all Christian souls, I pray God. God bye you.

       [*Exit*]

Laertes. Do you see this, O God?

King. Laertes, I must commune with your grief,
Or you deny me right. Go but apart,
Make choice of whom your wisest friends you will,
And they shall hear and judge 'twixt you and me.
If by direct or by collateral hand
They find us touched, we will our kingdom give,

Our crown, our life, and all that we call ours,
To you in satisfaction; but if not,
Be you content to lend your patience to us,
And we shall jointly labor with your soul
To give it due content.

Laertes.   Let this be so.
His means of death, his obscure funeral—
No trophy, sword, nor hatchment o'er his bones,
No noble rite nor formal ostentation—
Cry to be heard, as 'twere from heaven to earth,
That I must call't in question.

King.   So you shall;
And where th' offense is, let the great ax fall.
I pray you go with me.

     {Exeunt}

SCENE VI
WITHIN THE CASTLE

[Enter Horatio and others]

Horatio. What are they that would speak with me?

Gentleman. Seafaring men, sir. They say they have letters for you.

Horatio. Let them come in.

[Exit Attendant]

I do not know from what part of the world
I should be greeted, if not from Lord Hamlet.

[Enter Sailors]

Sailor. God bless you, sir.

Horatio. Let Him bless thee too.

Sailor. 'A shall, sir, an't please Him. There's a letter for you, sir—it came from th' ambassador that was bound for England—if your name be Horatio, as I am let to know it is.

Horatio. *[Reads the letter]* "Horatio, when thou shalt have overlooked this, give these fellows some means to the King. They have letters for him.

Ere we were two days old at sea, a pirate of very warlike appointment gave us chase. Finding ourselves too slow of sail, we put on a compelled valor, and in the grapple I boarded them. On the instant they got clear of our ship; so I alone became their prisoner. They have dealt with me like thieves of mercy, but they knew what they did: I am to do a good turn for them. Let the King have the letters I have sent, and repair thou to me with as much speed as thou wouldest fly death. I have words to speak in thine ear will make thee dumb; yet are they much too light for the bore of the matter. These good fellows will bring thee where I am. Rosencrantz and Guildenstern hold their course for England. Of them I have much to tell thee. Farewell.

He that thou knowest thine,

HAMLET."

Come, I will give you way for these your letters,
And do't the speedier that you may direct me
To him from whom you brought them.

[*Exeunt*]

{Enter King and Laertes}

King.   Now must your conscience my acquittance seal,
And you must put me in your heart for friend,
Sith you have heard, and with a knowing ear,
That he which hath your noble father slain
Pursued my life.

Laertes.   It well appears. But tell me
Why you proceeded not against these feats
So criminal and so capital in nature,
As by your safety, greatness, wisdom, all things else,
You mainly were stirred up.

King.   O, for two special reasons,
Which may to you perhaps seem much unsinewed,
But yet to me they're strong. The Queen his mother
Lives almost by his looks, and for myself—
My virtue or my plague, be it either which—
She is so conjunctive to my life and soul,
That, as the star moves not but in his sphere,
I could not but by her. The other motive

Why to a public count I might not go
Is the great love the general gender bear him,
Who, dipping all his faults in their affection,
Would, like the spring that turneth wood to stone,
Convert his gyves to graces; so that my arrows,
Too slightly timbered for so loud a wind,
Would have reverted to my bow again,
And not where I had aimed them.

Laertes. And so have I a noble father lost,
A sister driven into desp'rate terms,
Whose worth, if praises may go back again,
Stood challenger on mount of all the age
For her perfections. But my revenge will come.

King. Break not your sleeps for that. You must not think
That we are made of stuff so flat and dull
That we can let our beard be shook with danger,
And think it pastime. You shortly shall hear more.
I loved your father, and we love ourself,
And that, I hope, will teach you to imagine—
    [Enter a Messenger with letters]
How now? What news?

Messenger.	Letters, my lord, from Hamlet:
	These to your Majesty; this to the Queen.
King.	From Hamlet? Who brought them?
Messenger.	Sailors, my lord, they say; I saw them not.
	They were given me by Claudio; he received them
	Of him that brought them.
King.	Laertes, you shall hear them.—
	Leave us.

{*Exit Messenger*}

{*Reads*} "High and mighty, you shall know I am
set naked on your kingdom. Tomorrow shall I
beg leave to see your kingly eyes; when I shall
(first asking your pardon thereunto) recount
the occasion of my sudden and more strange
return.

HAMLET."

What should this mean? Are all the rest come back?
Or is it some abuse, and no such thing?

Laertes.	Know you the hand?
King.	'Tis Hamlet's character. "Naked"!
	And in a postscript here, he says "alone."
	Can you devise me?

Laertes. I am lost in it, my lord. But let him come.
It warms the very sickness in my heart
That I shall live and tell him to his teeth,
"Thus did'st thou."

King.   If it be so, Laertes
(As how should it be so? How otherwise?),
Will you be ruled by me?

Laertes.   Ay, my lord,
So you will not o'errule me to a peace.

King. To thine own peace. If he be now returned,
As checking at his voyage, and that he means
No more to undertake it, I will work him
To an exploit now ripe in my device,
Under the which he shall not choose but fall;
And for his death no wind of blame shall breathe,
But even his mother shall uncharge the practice
And call it accident.

Laertes.   My lord, I will be ruled;
The rather if you could devise it so
That I might be the organ.

King.   It falls right.
        You have been talked of since your travel much,
        And that in Hamlet's hearing, for a quality
        Wherein they say you shine. Your sum of parts
        Did not together pluck such envy from him
        As did that one, and that, in my regard,
        Of the unworthiest siege.

Laertes.   What part is that, my lord?

King.   A very riband in the cap of youth,
        Yet needful too, for youth no less becomes
        The light and careless livery that it wears
        Than settled age his sables and his weeds,
        Importing health and graveness. Two months since
        Here was a gentleman of Normandy.
        I have seen myself, and served against, the French,
        And they can well on horseback, but this gallant
        Had witchcraft in't. He grew unto his seat,
        And to such wondrous doing brought his horse
        As had he been incorpsed and deminatured
        With the brave beast. So far he topped my thought
        That I, in forgery of shapes and tricks,
        Come short of what he did.

Laertes.	A Norman was't?
King.	A Norman.
Laertes.	Upon my life, Lamord.
King.	The very same.
Laertes.	I know him well. He is the brooch indeed
	And gem of all the nation.
King.	He made confession of you,
	And gave you such a masterly report,
	For art and exercise in your defense,
	And for your rapier most especial,
	That he cried out 'twould be a sight indeed
	If one could match you. The scrimers of their nation
	He swore had neither motion, guard, nor eye,
	If you opposed them. Sir, this report of his
	Did Hamlet so envenom with his envy
	That he could nothing do but wish and beg
	Your sudden coming o'er to play with you.
	Now, out of this—
Laertes.	What out of this, my lord?

King.   Laertes, was your father dear to you?
        Or are you like the painting of a sorrow,
        A face without a heart?

Laertes.   Why ask you this?

King.   Not that I think you did not love your father,
        But that I know love is begun by time,
        And that I see, in passages of proof,
        Time qualifies the spark and fire of it.
        There lives within the very flame of love
        A kind of wick or snuff that will abate it,
        And nothing is at a like goodness still,
        For goodness, growing to a plurisy,
        Dies in his own too-much. That we would do
        We should do when we would, for this "would" changes,
        And hath abatements and delays as many
        As there are tongues, are hands, are accidents,
        And then this "should" is like a spendthrift sigh,
        That hurts by easing. But to the quick of th' ulcer—
        Hamlet comes back; what would you undertake
        To show yourself in deed your father's son
        More than in words?

Laertes.   To cut his throat i' th' church!

King. No place indeed should murder sanctuarize;
Revenge should have no bounds. But, good Laertes,
Will you do this? Keep close within your chamber.
Hamlet returned shall know you are come home.
We'll put on those shall praise your excellence
And set a double varnish on the fame
The Frenchman gave you, bring you in fine together
And wager on your heads. He, being remiss,
Most generous, and free from all contriving,
Will not peruse the foils, so that with ease,
Or with a little shuffling, you may choose
A sword unbated, and, in a pass of practice,
Requite him for your father.

Laertes.   I will do't,
And for that purpose I'll anoint my sword.
I bought an unction of a mountebank,
So mortal that, but dip a knife in it,
Where it draws blood, no cataplasm so rare,
Collected from all simples that have virtue
Under the moon, can save the thing from death
That is but scratched withal. I'll touch my point
With this contagion, that, if I gall him slightly,
It may be death.

King.   Let's further think of this,
Weigh what convenience both of time and means
May fit us to our shape. If this should fail,
And that our drift look through our bad performance,
'Twere better not assayed. Therefore this project
Should have a back or second, that might hold
If this did blast in proof. Soft, let me see.
We'll make a solemn wager on your cunnings—
I ha't!
When in your motion you are hot and dry—
As make your bouts more violent to that end—
And that he calls for drink, I'll have prepared him
A chalice for the nonce, whereon but sipping,
If he by chance escape your venomed stuck,
Our purpose may hold there.—But stay, what noise?
    {Enter Queen}

Queen. One woe doth tread upon another's heel.
So fast they follow. Your sister's drowned, Laertes.

Laertes. Drowned! O, where?

Queen. There is a willow grows askant the brook,
That shows his hoar leaves in the glassy stream:
Therewith fantastic garlands did she make
Of crowflowers, nettles, daisies, and long purples,
That liberal shepherds give a grosser name,
But our cold maids do dead men's fingers call them.
There on the pendent boughs her crownet weeds
Clamb'ring to hang, an envious sliver broke,
When down her weedy trophies and herself
Fell in the weeping brook. Her clothes spread wide,
And mermaidlike awhile they bore her up,
Which time she chanted snatches of old lauds,
As one incapable of her own distress,
Or like a creature native and indued
Unto that element. But long it could not be
Till that her garments, heavy with their drink,
Pulled the poor wretch from her melodious lay
To muddy death.

Laertes.   Alas, then she is drowned?

Queen. Drowned, drowned.

Laertes. Too much of water hast thou, poor Ophelia,
And therefore I forbid my tears; but yet
It is our trick; nature her custom holds,
Let shame say what it will: when these are gone,
The woman will be out. Adieu, my lord.
I have a speech o' fire, that fain would blaze,
But that this folly drowns it.

       [*Exit*]

King.   Let's follow, Gertrude.
How much I had to do to calm his rage!
Now fear I this will give it start again;
Therefore let's follow.

       [*Exeunt*]

ACT FIVE

SCENE I
A CHURCHYARD

[Enter two Clowns]

Clown.   Is she to be buried in Christian burial when she willfully seeks her own salvation?

Other.   I tell thee she is. Therefore make her grave straight. The crowner hath sate on her, and finds it Christian burial.

Clown.   How can that be, unless she drowned herself in her own defense?

Other.   Why, 'tis found so.

Clown.   It must be *se offendendo;* it cannot be else. For here lies the point: if I drown myself wittingly, it argues an act, and an act hath three branches —it is to act, to do, to perform. Argal, she drowned herself wittingly.

Other.   Nay, but hear you, Goodman Delver.

Clown. Give me leave. Here lies the water—good. Here stands the man—good. If the man go to this water and drown himself, it is, will he nill he, he goes; mark you that. But if the water come to him and drown him, he drowns not himself. Argal, he that is not guilty of his own death, shortens not his own life.

Other. But is this law?

Clown. Ay marry, is't—crowner's quest law.

Other. Will you ha' the truth on't? If this had not been a gentlewoman, she should have been buried out o' Christian burial.

Clown. Why, there thou say'st. And the more pity that great folk should have count'nance in this world to drown or hang themselves more than their even-Christen. Come, my spade. There is no ancient gentlemen but gard'ners, ditchers, and gravemakers. They hold up Adam's profession.

Other. Was he a gentleman?

Clown. 'A was the first that ever bore arms.

Other. Why, he had none.

Clown. What, art a heathen? How dost thou understand the Scripture? The Scripture says Adam digged. Could he dig without arms? I'll put another question to thee. If thou answerest me not to the purpose, confess thyself—

Other. Go to.

Clown. What is he that builds stronger than either the mason, the shipwright, or the carpenter?

Other. The gallowsmaker, for that frame outlives a thousand tenants.

Clown. I like thy wit well, in good faith. The gallows does well. But how does it well? It does well to those that do ill. Now thou dost ill to say the gallows is built stronger than the church. Argal, the gallows may do well to thee. To't again, come.

Other. Who builds stronger than a mason, a shipwright, or a carpenter?

Clown.	Ay, tell me that, and unyoke.
Other.	Marry, now I can tell.
Clown.	To't.
Other.	Mass, I cannot tell.

[Enter Hamlet and Horatio afar off]

Clown. Cudgel thy brains no more about it, for your
dull ass will not mend his pace with beating.
And when you are asked this question next, say
"a gravemaker." The houses he makes lasts till
doomsday. Go, get thee in, and fetch me a stoup
of liquor.

[Exit Other Clown]

[Sings]   In youth when I did love, did love,
Methought it was very sweet
To contract O the time for a my behove,
O, methought there was nothing meet.

Hamlet. Has this fellow no feeling of his business? 'A
sings in gravemaking.

Horatio. Custom hath made it in him a property of
easiness.

Hamlet. 'Tis e'en so. The hand of little employment
hath the daintier sense.

Clown. [*Sings*]   But age with his stealing steps
                      Hath clawed me in his clutch,
                      And hath shipped me into the land,
                      As if I had never been such.
      [*Throws up a skull*]

Hamlet. That skull had a tongue in it, and could sing
once. How the knave jowls it to the ground, as
if 'twere Cain's jawbone, that did the first murder! This might be the pate of a politician,
which this ass now o'erreaches, one that would
circumvent God, might it not?

Horatio. It might, my lord.

Hamlet. Or of a courtier, which could say "Good mor-
row, sweet lord! How dost thou, sweet lord?"
This might be my Lord Such-a-one, that praised
my Lord Such-a-one's horse when 'a went to
beg it, might it not?

Horatio. Ay, my lord.

Hamlet. Why, e'en so, and now my Lady Worm's, chapless, and knocked about the mazzard with a sexton's spade. Here's fine revolution, an we had the trick to see't. Did these bones cost no more the breeding but to play at loggets with them? Mine ache to think on't.

Clown. [*Sings*]   A pickax and a spade, a spade,
                 For and a shrouding sheet;
                 O, a pit of clay for to be made
                 For such a guest is meet.
        [*Throws up another skull*]

Hamlet. There's another. Why may not that be the skull of a lawyer? Where be his quiddities now, his quillities, his cases, his tenures, and his tricks? Why does he suffer this mad knave now to knock him about the sconce with a dirty shovel, and will not tell him of his action of battery? Hum! This fellow might be in's time a great buyer of land, with his statues, his recognizances, his fines, his double vouchers, his recov-

eries. Is this the fine of his fines, and the recov-
ery of his recoveries, to have his fine pate full of
fine dirt? Will his vouchers vouch him no more
of his purchases, and double ones too, than the
length and breadth of a pair of indentures? The
very conveyances of his lands will scarcely lie in
this box, and must th' inheritor himself have
no more, ha?

Horatio. Not a jot more, my lord.

Hamlet. Is not parchment made of sheepskins?

Horatio. Ay, my lord, and of calveskins too.

Hamlet. They are sheep and calves which seek out assurance in that. I will speak to this fellow. Whose
grave's this, sirrah?

Clown. Mine, sir.

[*Sings*]   O, a pit of clay for to be made
              For such a guest is meet.

Hamlet. I think it be thine indeed, for thou liest in't.

Clown. You lie out on't, sir, and therefore 'tis not yours.
For my part, I do not lie in't, yet it is mine.

Hamlet. Thou dost lie in't, to be in't and say it is thine. 'Tis for the dead, not for the quick; therefore thou liest.

Clown. 'Tis a quick lie, sir; 'twill away again from me to you.

Hamlet. What man dost thou dig it for?

Clown. For no man, sir.

Hamlet. What woman then?

Clown. For none neither.

Hamlet. Who is to be buried in't?

Clown. One that was a woman, sir; but, rest her soul, she's dead.

Hamlet. How absolute the knave is! We must speak by the card, or equivocation will undo us. By the Lord, Horatio, this three years I have took note of it, the age is grown so picked that the toe of the peasant comes so near the heel of the courtier he galls his kibe. How long hast thou been a gravemaker?

Clown. Of all the days i' th' year, I came to't that day that our last king Hamlet overcame Fortinbras.

Hamlet.	How long is that since?
Clown.	Cannot you tell that? Every fool can tell that. It was that very day that young Hamlet was born —he that is mad, and sent into England.
Hamlet.	Ay, marry, why was he sent into England?
Clown.	Why, because 'a was mad. 'A shall recover his wits there; or, if 'a do not, 'tis no great matter there.
Hamlet.	Why?
Clown.	'Twill not be seen in him there. There the men are as mad as he.
Hamlet.	How came he mad?
Clown.	Very strangely, they say.
Hamlet.	How strangely?
Clown.	Faith, e'en with losing his wits.
Hamlet.	Upon what ground?
Clown.	Why, here in Denmark. I have been sexton here, man and boy, thirty years.
Hamlet.	How long will a man lie i' th' earth ere he rot?

Clown. Faith, if 'a be not rotten before 'a die (as we have many pocky corses nowadays that will scarce hold the laying in), 'a will last you some eight year or nine year. A tanner will last you nine year.

Hamlet. Why he, more than another?

Clown. Why, sir, his hide is so tanned with his trade that 'a will keep out water a great while, and your water is a sore decayer of your whoreson dead body. Here's a skull now hath lien you i' th' earth three and twenty years.

Hamlet. Whose was it?

Clown. A whoreson mad fellow's it was. Whose do you think it was?

Hamlet. Nay, I know not.

Clown. A pestilence on him for a mad rogue! 'A poured a flagon of Rhenish on my head once. This same skull, sir, was, sir, Yorick's skull, the King's jester.

Hamlet. This?

Clown. E'en that.

Hamlet. Let me see. [*Takes the skull*] Alas, poor Yorick! I knew him, Horatio, a fellow of infinite jest, of most excellent fancy. He hath borne me on his back a thousand times. And now how abhorred in my imagination it is! My gorge rises at it. Here hung those lips that I have kissed I know not how oft. Where be your gibes now? Your gambols, your songs, your flashes of merriment that were wont to set the table on a roar? Not one now to mock your own grinning? Quite chapfall'n? Now get you to my lady's chamber, and tell her, let her paint an inch thick, to this favor she must come. Make her laugh at that. Prithee, Horatio, tell me one thing.

Horatio. What's that, my lord?

Hamlet. Dost thou think Alexander looked o' this fashion i 'th' earth?

Horatio. E'en so.

Hamlet. And smelt so? Pah ! [*Puts down the skull*]

Horatio. E'en so, my lord.

Hamlet. To what base uses we may return, Horatio! Why may not imagination trace the noble dust of Alexander till 'a find it stopping a bunghole?

Horatio. 'Twere to consider; too curiously, to consider so.

Hamlet. No, faith, not a jot, but to follow him thither
with modesty enough, and likelihood to lead it;
as thus: Alexander died, Alexander was buried,
Alexander returneth to dust; the dust is earth;
of earth we make loam; and why of that loam
whereto he was converted might they not stop a
beer barrel?
Imperious Caesar, dead and turned to clay,
Might stop a hole to keep the wind away.
O, that that earth which kept the world in awe
Should patch a wall t' expel the winter's flaw!
But soft, but soft awhile! Here comes the King.

     [Enter King, Queen, Laertes, and a coffin, with
      the Lords attendant and a Doctor of Divinity]

The Queen, the courtiers. Who is this they follow?
And with such maimèd rites? This doth betoken
The corse they follow did with desp'rate hand
Fordo it own life. 'Twas of some estate.
Couch we awhile, and mark.

     [Retires with Horatio]

Laertes.	What ceremony else?
Hamlet.	That is Laertes,
	A very noble youth. Mark.
Laertes.	What ceremony else?
Doctor.	Her obsequies have been as far enlarged
	As we have warranty. Her death was doubtful,
	And, but that great command o'ersways the order,
	She should in ground unsanctified been lodged
	Till the last trumpet. For charitable prayers,
	Shards, flints, and pebbles should be thrown on her.
	Yet here she is allowed her virgin crants,
	Her maiden strewments, and the bringing home
	Of bell and burial.
Laertes.	Must there no more be done?
Doctor.	No more be done.
	We should profane the service of the dead
	To sing a requiem and such rest to her
	As to peace-parted souls.

Laertes.   Lay her i' th' earth,
And from her fair and unpolluted flesh
May violets spring! I tell thee, churlish priest,
A minist'ring angel shall my sister be
When thou liest howling!

Hamlet.   What, the fair Ophelia?

Queen.   Sweets to the sweet! Farewell.
          [Scatters flowers]
I hoped thou shouldst have been my Hamlet's wife.
I thought thy bride bed to have decked, sweet maid,
And not have strewed thy grave.

Laertes.   O, treble woe
Fall ten times treble on that cursèd head
Whose wicked deed thy most ingenious sense
Deprived thee of! Hold off the earth awhile,
Till I have caught her once more in mine arms.
          [Leaps in the grave]
Now pile your dust upon the quick and dead
Till of this flat a mountain you have made
T'o'ertop old Pelion or the skyish head
Of blue Olympus.

Hamlet. [*Coming forward*] What is he whose grief
Bears such an emphasis, whose phrase of sorrow
Conjures the wand'ring stars, and makes them stand
Like wonder-wounded hearers? This is I,
Hamlet the Dane.

Laertes.   The devil take thy soul!
   [*Grapples with him*]

Hamlet. Thou pray'st not well.
I prithee take thy fingers from my throat,
For, though I am not splenitive and rash,
Yet have I in me something dangerous,
Which let thy wisdom fear. Hold off thy hand.

King. Pluck them asunder.

Queen.   Hamlet, Hamlet!

All. Gentlemen!

Horatio.   Good my lord, be quiet.
   [*Attendants part them*]

Hamlet. Why, I will fight with him upon this theme
Until my eyelids will no longer wag.

Queen. O my son, what theme?

Hamlet.	I loved Ophelia. Forty thousand brothers
	Could not with all their quantity of love
	Make up my sum. What wilt thou do for her?
King.	O, he is mad, Laertes.
Queen.	For love of God forbear him.
Hamlet.	'Swounds, show me what thou't do.
	Woo't weep? Woo't fight? Woo't fast? Woo't tear thyself?
	Woo't drink up eisel? Eat a crocodile?
	I'll do't. Dost thou come here to whine?
	To outface me with leaping in her grave?
	Be buried quick with her, and so will I.
	And if thou prate of mountains, let them throw
	Millions of acres on us, till our ground,
	Singeing his pate against the burning zone,
	Make Ossa like a wart! Nay, an thou'lt mouth,
	I'll rant as well as thou.
Queen.	This is mere madness;
	And thus a while the fit will work on him.
	Anon, as patient as the female dove
	When that her golden couplets are disclosed,
	His silence will sit drooping.

Hamlet.   Here you, sir.

What is the reason that you use me thus?

I loved you ever. But it is no matter.

Let Hercules himself do what he may,

The cat will mew, and dog will have his day.

King.   I pray thee, good Horatio, wait upon him.

        [Exit Hamlet and Horatio]

[To Laertes] Strengthen your patience in our last night's speech.

We'll put the matter to the present push.

Good Gertrude, set some watch over your son.

This grave shall have a living monument.

An hour of quiet shortly shall we see;

Till then in patience our proceeding be.

        [Exeunt]

[Enter Hamlet and Horatio]

Hamlet.   So much for this, sir; now shall you see the other.

          You do remember all the circumstance?

Horatio.   Remember it, my lord!

Hamlet.   Sir, in my heart there was a kind of fighting

          That would not let me sleep. Methought I lay

          Worse than the mutines in the bilboes. Rashly

          (And praised be rashness for it) let us know,

          Our indiscretion sometime serves us well

          When our deep plots do pall, and that should learn us

          There's a divinity that shapes our ends,

          Rough-hew them how we will.

Horatio.   That is most certain.

Hamlet.   Up from my cabin,

          My sea gown scarfed about me, in the dark

          Groped I to find out them, had my desire,

          Fingered their packet, and in fine withdrew

          To mine own room again, making so bold,

          My fears forgetting manners, to unseal

Their grand commission; where I found, Horatio—
Ah, royal knavery!—an exact command,
Larded with many several sorts of reasons,
Importing Denmark's health, and England's too,
With, ho, such bugs and goblins in my life,
That on the supervise, no leisure bated,
No, not to stay the grinding of the ax,
My head should be struck off.

Horatio.   Is't possible?

Hamlet. Here's the commission; read it at more leisure.
But wilt thou hear now how I did proceed?

Horatio. I beseech you.

Hamlet. Being thus benetted round with villains,
Or I could make a prologue to my brains,
They had begun the play. I sat me down,
Devised a new commission, wrote it fair.
I once did hold it, as our statists do,
A baseness to write fair, and labored much
How to forget that learning, but, sir, now
It did me yeoman's service. Wilt thou know
Th' effect of what I wrote?

Horatio.	Ay, good my lord.
Hamlet.	An earnest conjuration from the King,
	As England was his faithful tributary,
	As love between them like the palm might flourish,
	As peace should still her wheaten garland wear
	And stand a comma 'tween their amities,
	And many suchlike as's of great charge,
	That on the view and knowing of these contents,
	Without debatement further, more or less,
	He should those bearers put to sudden death,
	Not shriving time allowed.
Horatio.	How was this sealed?
Hamlet.	Why, even in that was heaven ordinant.
	I had my father's signet in my purse,
	Which was the model of that Danish seal,
	Folded the writ up in the form of th' other,
	Subscribed it, gave't th' impression, placed it safely,
	The changeling never known. Now, the next day
	Was our sea fight, and what to this was sequent
	Thou knowest already.

Horatio.	So Guildenstern and Rosencrantz go to't.
Hamlet.	Why, man, they did make love to this employment.
	They are not near my conscience; their defeat
	Does by their own insinuation grow.
	'Tis dangerous when the baser nature comes
	Between the pass and fell incensèd points
	Of mighty opposites.
Horatio.	Why, what a king is this!
Hamlet.	Does it not, think thee, stand me now upon—
	He that hath killed my king, and whored my mother,
	Popped in between th' election and my hopes,
	Thrown out his angle for my proper life,
	And with such coz'nage—is't not perfect conscience
	To quit him with this arm? And is't not to be damned
	To let this canker of our nature come
	In further evil?
Horatio.	It must be shortly known to him from England
	What is the issue of the business there.

Hamlet.   It will be short; the interim's mine,
          And a man's life's no more than to say "one."
          But I am very sorry, good Horatio,
          That to Laertes I forgot myself,
          For by the image of my cause I see
          The portraiture of his. I'll court his favors.
          But sure the bravery of his grief did put me
          Into a tow'ring passion.

Horatio.   Peace, who comes here?
                    [Enter young Osric, a courtier]

Osric.   Your lordship is right welcome back to Denmark.

Hamlet.   I humbly thank you, sir. [Aside to Horatio] Dost
          know this waterfly?

Horatio. [Aside to Hamlet] No, my good lord.

Hamlet.   [Aside to Horatio] Thy state is the more gracious,
          for 'tis a vice to know him. He hath much land,
          and fertile. Let a beast be lord of beasts, and his
          crib shall stand at the king's mess. 'Tis a chough,
          but, as I say, spacious in the possession of dirt.

Osric.   Sweet lord, if your lordship were at leisure, I
          should impart a thing to you from his Majesty.

Hamlet. I will receive it, sir, with all diligence of spirit. Put your bonnet to his right use. 'Tis for the head.

Osric. I thank your lordship, it is very hot.

Hamlet. No, believe me, 'tis very cold; the wind is northerly.

Osric. It is indifferent cold, my lord, indeed.

Hamlet. But yet methinks it is very sultry and hot for my complexion.

Osric. Exceedingly, my lord; it is very sultry, as 'twere —I cannot tell how. But, my lord, his Majesty bade me signify to you that 'a has laid a great wager on your head. Sir, this is the matter—

Hamlet. I beseech you remember.

[*Hamlet moves him to put on his hat*]

Osric. Nay, good my lord; for my ease, in good faith. Sir, here is newly come to court Laertes—believe me, an absolute gentleman, full of most excellent differences, of very soft society and great showing. Indeed, to speak feelingly of him, he is the card or calendar of gentry; for you shall find in him the continent of what part a gentleman would see.

Hamlet. Sir, his definement suffers no perdition in you, though, I know, to divide him inventorially would dozy th' arithmetic of memory, and yet but yaw neither in respect of his quick sail. But, in the verity of extolment, I take him to be a soul of great article, and his infusion of such dearth and rareness as, to make true diction of him, his semblable is his mirror, and who else would trace him, his umbrage, nothing more.

Osric. Your lordship speaks most infallibly of him.

Hamlet. The concernancy, sir? Why do we wrap the gentleman in our more rawer breath?

Osric. Sir?

Horatio. Is't not possible to understand in another tongue? You will to't, sir, really.

Hamlet. What imports the nomination of this gentleman?

Osric. Of Laertes?

Horatio. *[Aside to Hamlet]* His purse is empty already. All's golden words are spent.

Hamlet. Of him, sir.

Osric. I know you are not ignorant—

Hamlet. I would you did, sir; yet, in faith, if you did, it would not much approve me. Well, sir?

Osric. You are not ignorant of what excellence Laertes is—

Hamlet. I dare not confess that, lest I should compare with him in excellence; but to know a man well were to know himself.

Osric. I mean, sir, for his weapon; but in the imputation laid on him by them, in his meed he's unfellowed.

Hamlet. What's his weapon?

Osric. Rapier and dagger.

Hamlet. That's two of his weapons—but well.

Osric. The King, sir, hath wagered with him six Barbary horses, against the which he has impawned, as I take it, six French rapiers and poniards, with their assigns, as girdle, hangers, and so. Three of the carriages, in faith, are very dear to fancy, very responsive to the hilts, most delicate carriages, and of very liberal conceit.

Hamlet. What call you the carriages?

Horatio. [*Aside to Hamlet*] I knew you must be edified by the margent ere you had done.

Osric. The carriages, sir, are the hangers.

Hamlet. The phrase would be more germane to the matter if we could carry a cannon by our sides. I would it might be hangers till then. But on! Six Barbary horses against six French swords, their assigns, and three liberal-conceited carriages—that's the French bet against the Danish. Why is this all impawned, as you call it?

Osric. The King, sir, hath laid, sir, that in a dozen passes between yourself and him he shall not exceed you three hits; he hath laid on twelve for nine, and it would come to immediate trial if your lordship would vouchsafe the answer.

Hamlet. How if I answer no?

Osric. I mean, my lord, the opposition of your person in trial.

Hamlet. Sir, I will walk here in the hall. If it please his Majesty, it is the breathing time of day with me. Let the foils be brought, the gentleman willing, and the King hold his purpose, I will win for him an I can; if not, I will gain nothing but my shame and the odd hits.

Osric. Shall I deliver you e'en so?

Hamlet. To this effect, sir, after what flourish your nature will.

Osric. I commend my duty to your lordship.

Hamlet. Yours, yours. [*Exit Osric*] He does well to commend it himself; there are no tongues else for's turn.

Horatio. This lapwing runs away with the shell on his head.

Hamlet. 'A did comply, sir, with his dug before 'a sucked it. Thus has he, and many more of the same breed that I know the drossy age dotes on, only got the tune of the time and, out of an habit of encounter, a kind of yeasty collection, which carries them through and through the most fanned and winnowed opinions; and do but blow them to their trial, the bubbles are out.

Lord. My lord, his Majesty commended him to you by young Osric, who brings back to him that you attend him in the hall. He sends to know if your pleasure hold to play with Laertes, or that you will take longer time.

Hamlet. I am constant to my purposes; they follow the King's pleasure. If his fitness speaks, mine is ready; now or whensoever, provided I be so able as now.

Lord. The King and Queen and all are coming down.

Hamlet. In happy time.

Lord. The Queen desires you to use some gentle entertainment to Laertes before you fall to play.

Hamlet. She well instructs me.

[Exit Lord]

Horatio. You will lose this wager, my lord.

Hamlet. I do not think so. Since he went into France I have been in continual practice. I shall win at the odds. But thou wouldst not think how ill all's here about my heart. But it is no matter.

Horatio. Nay, good my lord —

Hamlet. It is but foolery, but it is such a kind of gain-giving as would perhaps trouble a woman.

Horatio. If your mind dislike anything, obey it. I will forestall their repair hither and say you are not fit.

Hamlet. Not a whit, we defy augury. There is special providence in the fall of a sparrow. If it be now, 'tis not to come; if it be not to come, it will be now; if it be not now, yet it will come. The readiness is all. Since no man of aught he leaves knows, what is't to leave betimes? Let be.

> [*A table prepared. Enter Trumpets, Drums, and Officers with cushions; King, Queen, Osric, and all the State, with foils, daggers, and stoups of wine borne in; and Laertes*]

King. Come, Hamlet, come, and take this hand from me.

{The King puts Laertes' hand into Hamlet's}

Hamlet. Give me your pardon, sir. I have done you wrong,
But pardon't, as you are a gentleman.
This presence knows, and you must needs have heard,
How I am punished with a sore distraction.
What I have done
That might your nature, honor, and exception
Roughly awake, I here proclaim was madness.
Was't Hamlet wronged Laertes? Never Hamlet.
If Hamlet from himself be ta'en away,
And when he's not himself does wrong Laertes,
Then Hamlet does it not, Hamlet denies it.
Who does it then? His madness. If't be so,
Hamlet is of the faction that is wronged;
His madness is poor Hamlet's enemy.
Sir, in this audience,
Let my disclaiming from a purposed evil
Free me so far in your most generous thoughts
That I have shot my arrow o'er the house
And hurt my brother.

Laertes.   I am satisfied in nature,
Whose motive in this case should stir me most
To my revenge. But in my terms of honor
I stand aloof, and will no reconcilement
Till by some elder masters of known honor
I have a voice and precedent of peace
To keep my name ungored. But till that time
I do receive your offered love like love,
And will not wrong it.

Hamlet.   I embrace it freely,
And will this brother's wager frankly play.
Give us the foils. Come on.

Laertes.   Come, one for me.

Hamlet. I'll be your foil, Laertes. In mine ignorance
Your skill shall, like a star i' th' darkest night,
Stick fiery off indeed.

Laertes.   You mock me, sir.

Hamlet. No, by this hand.

King. Give them the foils, young Osric. Cousin Hamlet,
You know the wager?

Hamlet.	Very well, my lord.
	Your grace has laid the odds o' th' weaker side.
King.	I do not fear it, I have seen you both;
	But since he is bettered, we have therefore odds.
Laertes.	This is too heavy; let me see another.
Hamlet.	This likes me well. These foils have all a length?
	{*Prepare to play*}
Osric.	Ay, my good lord.
King.	Set me the stoups of wine upon that table.
	If Hamlet give the first or second hit,
	Or quit in answer of the third exchange,
	Let all the battlements their ordnance fire.
	The King shall drink to Hamlet's better breath,
	And in the cup an union shall he throw
	Richer than that which four successive kings
	In Denmark's crown have worn. Give me the cups,
	And let the kettle to the trumpet speak,
	The trumpet to the cannoneer without,
	The cannons to the heavens, the heaven to earth,
	"Now the King drinks to Hamlet." Come, begin
	{*Trumpets the while*}
	And you, the judges, bear a wary eye.

Hamlet.	Come on, sir.
Laertes.	Come, my lord. {*They play*}
Hamlet.	One.
Laertes.	No.
Hamlet.	Judgment?
Osric.	A hit, a very palpable hit.

{*Drum, trumpets, and shot. Flourish; a piece goes off*}

Laertes.	Well, again.
King.	Stay, give me drink. Hamlet, this pearl is thine. Here's to thy health. Give him the cup.
Hamlet.	I'll play this bout first; set it by awhile. Come. {*They play*} Another hit. What say you?
Laertes.	A touch, a touch; I do confess't.
King.	Our son shall win.
Queen.	He's fat, and scant of breath. Here, Hamlet, take my napkin, rub thy brows. The Queen carouses to thy fortune, Hamlet.
Hamlet.	Good madam!
King.	Gertrude, do not drink.
Queen.	I will, my lord; I pray you pardon me. {*Drinks*}
King.	{*Aside*} It is the poisoned cup; it is too late.

Hamlet.	I dare not drink yet, madam—by and by.
Queen.	Come, let me wipe thy face.
Laertes.	My lord, I'll hit him now.
King.	I do not think't.
Laertes.	[*Aside*] And yet it is almost against my conscience.
Hamlet.	Come for the third, Laertes. You do but dally.
	I pray you pass with your best violence;
	I am sure you make a wanton of me.
Laertes.	Say you so? Come on. [*They play*]
Osric.	Nothing neither way.
Laertes.	Have at you now!
	[*In scuffling they change rapiers, and both are wounded*]
King.	Part them. They are incensed.
Hamlet.	Nay, come—again!
	[*The Queen falls*]
Osric.	Look to the Queen there, ho!
Horatio.	They bleed on both sides. How is it, my lord?
Osric.	How is't, Laertes?
Laertes.	Why, as a woodcock to mine own springe, Osric.
	I am justly killed with mine own treachery.
Hamlet.	How does the Queen?

King.	She sounds to see them bleed.
Queen.	No, no, the drink, the drink! O my dear Hamlet!
	The drink, the drink! I am poisoned.
	{Dies}
Hamlet.	O villainy! Ho! Let the door be locked.
	Treachery! Seek it out.
	{Laertes falls}
Laertes.	It is here, Hamlet. Hamlet, thou art slain;
	No med'cine in the world can do thee good.
	In thee there is not half an hour's life.
	The treacherous instrument is in thy hand,
	Unbated and envenomed. The foul practice
	Hath turned itself on me. Lo, here I lie,
	Never to rise again. Thy mother's poisoned.
	I can no more. The King, the King's to blame.
Hamlet.	The point envenomed too?
	Then, venom, to thy work.
	{Hurts the King}
All.	Treason! Treason!
King.	O, yet defend me, friends. I am but hurt.
Hamlet.	Here, thou incestuous, murd'rous, damnèd Dane,
	Drink off this potion. Is thy union here?
	Follow my mother.
	{King dies}

Laertes.   He is justly served.
It is a poison tempered by himself.
Exchange forgiveness with me, noble Hamlet.
Mine and my father's death come not upon thee,
Nor thine on me!
          {*Dies*}
Hamlet.   Heaven make thee free of it! I follow thee.
I am dead, Horatio. Wretched Queen, adieu!
You that look pale and tremble at this chance,
That are but mutes or audience to this act,
Had I but time (as this fell sergeant, Death,
Is strict in his arrest) O, I could tell you—
But let it be. Horatio, I am dead;
Thou livest; report me and my cause aright
To the unsatisfied.
Horatio.   Never believe it.
I am more an antique Roman than a Dane.
Here's yet some liquor left.

Hamlet.	As th' art a man,
	Give me the cup. Let go. By heaven, I'll ha't!
	O God, Horatio, what a wounded name,
	Things standing thus unknown, shall live behind me!
	If thou didst ever hold me in thy heart,
	Absent thee from felicity awhile,
	And in this harsh world draw thy breath in pain,
	To tell my story.

        {A march afar off. Exit Osric}

                      What warlike noise is this?

        {Enter Osric}

Osric.	Young Fortinbras, with conquest come from Poland,
	To th' ambassadors of England gives
	This warlike volley.
Hamlet.	O, I die, Horatio!
	The potent poison quite o'ercrows my spirit.
	I cannot live to hear the news from England,
	But I do prophesy th' election lights
	On Fortinbras. He has my dying voice.
	So tell him, with th' occurrents, more and less,
	Which have solicited—the rest is silence.

        {Dies}

Horatio. Now cracks a noble heart. Good night, sweet Prince,
And flights of angels sing thee to thy rest.
{March within}
Why does the drum come hither?
{Enter Fortinbras, with Ambassadors
with Drum, Colors, and Attendants}
Fortinbras. Where is this sight?
Horatio. What is it you would see?
If aught of woe or wonder, cease your search.
Fortinbras. This quarry cries on havoc. O proud Death,
What feast is toward in thine eternal cell
That thou so many princes at a shot
So bloodily hast struck?
Ambassador. The sight is dismal;
And our affairs from England come too late.
The ears are senseless that should give us hearing
To tell him his commandment is fulfilled,
That Rosencrantz and Guildenstern are dead.
Where should we have our thanks?

Horatio.   Not from his mouth,
Had it th' ability of life to thank you.
He never gave commandment for their death.
But since, so jump upon this bloody question,
You from the Polack wars, and you from England,
Are here arrived, give order that these bodies
High on a stage be placèd to the view,
And let me speak to th' yet unknowing world
How these things came about. So shall you hear
Of carnal, bloody, and unnatural acts,
Of accidental judgments, casual slaughters,
Of deaths put on by cunning and forced cause,
And, in this upshot, purposes mistook
Fall'n on th' inventors' heads. All this can I
Truly deliver.

Fortinbras.   Let us haste to hear it,
And call the noblest to the audience.
For me, with sorrow I embrace my fortune.
I have some rights of memory in this kingdom,
Which now to claim my vantage doth invite me.

Horatio.   Of that I shall have also cause to speak,
And from his mouth whose voice will draw on more.
But let this same be presently performed,
Even while men's minds are wild, lest more mischance
On plots and errors happen.

Fortinbras.   Let four captains
Bear Hamlet like a soldier to the stage,
For he was likely, had he been put on,
To have proved most royal; and for his passage
The soldiers' music and the rite of war
Speak loudly for him.
Take up the bodies. Such a sight as this
Becomes the field, but here shows much amiss.
Go, bid the soldiers shoot.

*{Exeunt marching; after which
a peal of ordnance are shot off}*

FINIS

EPILOGUE—*William Hazlitt*

This is that Hamlet the Dane, whom we read of in our youth, and whom we may be said almost to remember in our after-years; he who made that famous soliloquy on life, who gave the advice to the players, who thought "this goodly frame, the earth, a steril promontory, and this brave o'er-hanging firmament, the air, this majestical roof fretted with golden fire, a foul and pestilent congregation of vapors"; whom "man delighted not, nor woman neither"; he who talked with the gravediggers, and moralized on Yorick's skull; the schoolfellow of Rosencrantz and Guildenstern at Wittenberg; the friend of Horatio; the lover of Ophelia; he that was mad and sent to England; the slow avenger of his father's death; who lived at the court of Horwendillus five hundred years before we were born, but all whose thoughts we seem to know as well as we do our own, because we have read them in Shakespear.

Hamlet is a name; his speeches and sayings but the idle coinage of the poet's brain. What then, are they not real? They are as real as our own thoughts. Their reality is in the reader's mind. It is *we* who are Hamlet. This play has a prophetic truth, which is above that of history. Whoever has become thoughtful and melancholy through his own mishaps or those of others; whoever has borne about with him the clouded brow of reflection, and thought himself "too much i' th' sun"; whoever has seen the golden lamp of day dimmed by envious mists rising in his own breast, and could find in the world before him only a dull blank with nothing left remarkable in it; whoever has known the "pangs of despised love, the insolence of office, or the spurns which patient merit of the unworthy takes"; he who has felt his mind sink within him, and sadness cling to his heart like a malady, who has had his hopes blighted and his youth staggered by the apparitions of strange things; who cannot be well at ease while he sees evil hovering near him like a specter; whose powers of action have been eaten up by thought, he to whom the universe seems infinite, and himself nothing; whose bitterness of soul makes him careless of consequences, and who goes to a play as his best resource to shove off, to a second remove, the evils of life by a mock representation of them—this is the true Hamlet.

We have been so used to this tragedy that we hardly know how to criticize it any more than we should know how to describe our own faces. But we must make such observations as we can. It is the one of Shakespear's plays that we think of the oftenest, because it abounds most in striking reflections on human life, and because the distresses of Hamlet are transferred, by the turn of his mind, to the general account of humanity. Whatever happens to him we apply to ourselves, because he applies it to himself as a means of general reasoning. He is a great moralizer; and what makes him worth attending to is that he moralizes on his own feelings and experience. He is not a commonplace pedant. If Lear is distinguished by the greatest depth of passion, Hamlet is the most remarkable for the ingenuity, originality, and unstudied development of character. Shakespear had more magnanimity than any other poet, and he has shown more of it in this play than in any other. There is no attempt to force an interest: everything is left for time and circumstances to unfold. The attention is excited without effort, the incidents succeed each other as matters of course, the characters think and speak and act just as they might do if left entirely to themselves. There is no set purpose, no straining at a point. The observations are suggested by the passing scene—the gusts of passion come and go like sounds of music borne on the wind. The whole play is an exact transcript of what might be supposed to have taken place at the court of Denmark, at the remote period of time fixed upon before the modern refinements in morals and manners were heard of. It would have been interesting enough to have been admitted as a bystander in such a scene, at such a time, to have heard and witnessed something of what was going on. But here we are more than spectators. We have not only "the outward pageants and the signs of grief," but "we have that within which passes show." We read the thoughts of the heart, we catch the passions living as they rise. Other dramatic writers give us very fine versions and paraphrases of nature; but Shakespear, together with his own comments, gives us the original text, that we may judge for ourselves. This is a very great advantage.

The character of Hamlet stands quite by itself. It is not a character marked by strength of will or even of passion, but by refinement of thought and sentiment. Hamlet is as little of the hero as a man can well be; but he is a young and princely novice, full of high enthusiasm and quick sensibility—the sport of circumstances, questioning with fortune and refining on his own feelings, and forced from the natural bias of his disposition by the strangeness of his situation. He seems incapable of deliberate action, and is only hurried into extremities on the spur of the occasion, when he has no time to reflect, as in the scene where he kills Polonius, and again, where he alters the letters which Rosencrantz and Guildenstern are taking with them to England, purporting his death. At other times, when he is most bound to act, he remains puzzled, undecided, and skeptical, dallies with his purposes, till the occasion is lost, and finds out some pretense to relapse into indolence and thoughtfulness again. For this reason he refuses to kill the King when he is at his prayers, and by a refinement in malice, which is in truth only an excuse for his own want of resolution, defers his revenge to a more fatal opportunity, when he shall be engaged in some act "that has no relish of salvation in it."

He kneels and prays,
And now I'll do't, and so he goes to heaven,
And so am I reveng'd: *that would be scann'd.*
He kill'd my father, and for that,
I, his sole son, send him to heaven.
Why, this is reward, not revenge.
Up sword and know thou a more horrid time,
When he is drunk, asleep, or in a rage.

He is the prince of philosophical speculators; and because he cannot have his revenge perfect, according to the most refined idea his wish can form, he declines it altogether. So he scruples to trust the suggestions of the ghost, contrives the scene of the play to have surer proof of his uncle's guilt, and then rests satisfied with this confirmation of his suspicions, and the success of his experiment, instead of acting upon it. Yet he is sensible of his own weakness, taxes himself with it, and tries to reason himself out of it....

Still he does nothing; and this very speculation on his own infirmity only affords him another occasion for indulging it. It is not from any want of attachment to his father or of abhorrence of his murder that Hamlet is thus dilatory, but it is more to his taste to indulge his imagination in reflecting upon the enormity of the crime and refining on his schemes of vengeance, than to put them into immediate practice. His ruling passion is to think, not to act: and any vague pretext that flatters this propensity instantly diverts him from his previous purposes....

COLOPHON

Typography by Composing Room + Graphic Arts Typographers, Inc. The text is set in 14 pt. Cloister Bold with 12 pt. Italics. All display copy is set photomechanically in ATF Cloister Bold. Complete page negatives, ready for platemaking have been prepared. Printed Offset by Thompson Lithographic Associates Inc. on a 60-inch Harris 2-color press using custom ball grain aluminum wipe-on plates. The paper manufactured by Finch, Pruyn & Company, Inc. is Finch Title 95, Laid Finish, Opaque White, Basis 70. Binding by Sendor Bindery, Inc. Three-piece Holliston Cloth, Dull Black Levant 7X back, and Kingston Natural 35398. The endpapers are Elephant Hide Number 25. Illustrations by Jack Wolfgang Beck. Design by Daniel Haberman.

HAMLET:
WILLIAM SHAKESPEARE

.